LIVING LIFE, LIVING FAITH

by

Aaron Grube & Edward Grube

Concordia
Publishing House

Published by Concordia Publishing House
3558 S. Jefferson Avenue, St. Louis, MO 63118-3968
1-800-325-3040 • www.cph.org

LIBRARY OF CONGRESS CATALOGING-IN-PUBLICATION DATA

Names: Grube, Aaron, author. | Grube, Edward C., 1947- author.
Title: Living life, living faith / by Aaron Grube & Edward Grube.
Description: St. Louis, MO : Concordia Publishing House, [2016] |
Includes bibliographical references and index.
Identifiers: LCCN 2016013379 (print) | LCCN 2016015100 (ebook) |
ISBN 9780758654762 (alk. paper) | ISBN 9780758654779 ()
Subjects: LCSH: Christian life.
Classification: LCC BV4501.3 .G79 2016 (print) | LCC BV4501.3
(ebook) | DDC 248.8/34--dc23
LC record available at https://lccn.loc.gov/2016013379

1 2 3 4 5 6 7 8 9 10 25 24 23 22 21 20 19 18 17 16

To Renee and Andie, both wives and mother—life's best teachers, whose love and care have nurtured us through many of life's lessons.

Table of Contents

Introduction

What lies ahead? Your future might include starting a new job or changing careers, dealing with relationships, relocating to a new city, and a host of other challenges. Father and son author team—Edward and Aaron Grube—collaborated on each of the fifty-two *Living Life, Living Faith* essays in this book. Aaron shares his real-life experiences while Ed includes his fatherly and biblical advice in a unique and engaging style. As you read, you will discover that the issues these two address are the same you may be facing in your own life as well. Each lesson includes the calming reassurance of God's continual love and concern for the challenges you face now and in the future.

Aaron (Son)
Life Stories

Aaron and wife, Andie—along with 2 dogs, 2 cats, and 2 rabbits—live in Kalamazoo, MI where he serves Zion Lutheran Church as Director of Christian Education. Aaron ran into a lot of things when he was little which sparked his uncanny superhuman balance, as well as creating a lot of good (embarrassing) stories to share!

Ed (Dad)
Reflections

Ed and Renee Grube live in Addison, Illinois. After many years as a school principal and administrator, Ed now serves as Director of Publications & Communications for Lutheran Education Association. Neighbors reportedly ask Ed not to practice accordion with the windows open.

1

Change Happens

Acts 8–9

Congratulations! Your days of running to class, working on that research paper, and studying for exams have finally paid off. Welcome to the world of waking up early for work, settling down, and constructing a career. At least that is the plan, right?

Since kindergarten, the life you have known has involved a consistent routine of studying, learning, and being tested. Think about it. As you progressed through elementary and middle school, your routine became less structured. High school put a little more responsibility on you, and in college you were most likely able to set your own schedule. Life as you know it is about to change.

Change can be difficult. It can be uncomfortable. But along with change comes growth and opportunity. Most people need to see the benefits of the changes they are encountering in order to see the changes as worthwhile. How have you dealt with changes in your life? Do you embrace them or run from them? Do you whine and complain or do you make adjustments to fully engage the alterations?

I remember when my wife, Andie, and I got our puppy. Our Blue Heeler/Great Dane mix certainly was a handful in our small, two-bedroom apartment. Being confined to a small space, the not-so-medium-size dog—as he was originally described—was quickly finding creative ways to utilize his surroundings. One time when we had some friends over, Harvey noticed there was no room for him on the couch, so he decided to lie on the back of the couch like a cat! He was doing just fine adjusting to his large size . . . but we were not. Although, it was not too bad until he decided that our bed was also his bed!

Getting a puppy was a life-changing event. I had to stop at home for lunch, plan on walking time if we wanted to get any sleep at all, and we could no longer spend a night out of town without finding a "sitter." We added more responsibility and structure to our schedule—to this day, Harvey tells me when it is five o'clock feeding time. But there were also benefits to the change. The dog provides comfort and joy, an outlet to show love and care. The benefits are well worth the change in lifestyle.

One famous example of change in the Bible is good old Saul . . . err, Paul. Saul was a Pharisee, a religious man. Yet, Saul persecuted the early Christians. Acts 8:1 even says, "Saul approved of his [Stephen's] execution." Saul's life probably consisted of a routine of religious practices, breathing out murderous threats, and "defending" his faith by persecuting others. On the road to Damascus, Saul's life abruptly changed! His agenda changed, his lifestyle changed, and eventually even his name changed, all because of his encounter with Jesus.

Do you remember when your life changed—when you first realized what Jesus did for you on the cross? That single act by Christ destroyed the devil's claim on you and freed you from sin's eternal consequence.

Your life is about to change. Your routines, habits, and schedules will undergo makeovers. Whether you have a new job lined up, are moving back home, or have no clue what your next step is, use the changes that are about to occur as an opportunity. Chances are you will be meeting new people and starting new relationships! You will be experiencing different stressors such as finances, culture, and work. Society will finally see you as an adult, but expectations will also increase. Whatever changes you are going through now and whatever you encounter in the future, be sure to stay in relationship with God. Dwell on His Word and grow closer to Him and fellow Christians. Change can cause a lot of instability in life. God is the anchor that will never fail you. Rely on Him and trust in His plan for your life.

Reflection

Change happens whether you control it or not—and you often can't even begin to imagine the effect it will ultimately have on your life. If nothing else, this fact can keep you humble. And the older you get, the more opportunities you have to be humbled!

Take cell phones. Although the parade of upgrades is cause to keep a twinkle in marketers' eyes, most newer phones look much like previous models. But can you imagine what they will look like in fifty years? Probably haven't thought about it much, right?

Fifty years ago, most telephones were black and heavy, certainly not portable beyond the cord that connected it to a wall receptacle. As for making a connection, you stuck your finger in a rotary dial and spun it around for each digit in the phone number. (Hmm, I guess phones were "digital" back then!) The rotary phone eventually evolved into push buttons, but the basic design was the same. I never dreamed what phones would look and operate like they do today.

Fifty years from now, what will you say about the phones of yesteryear? You'll probably say, "Phones? I've heard of them—seen them in museums. But how did people survive without iComs? I couldn't! Though I hope the chip doesn't leave a scar!"

Change is ancient—just imagine Adam and Eve upon their departure from the garden. Perfect bliss and harmony became more like life as we know it today after their split-second lapse in judgment. Changes brought about by sin are often most difficult to manage. Good thing God had another change in mind—the change from condemnation to redemption through the life, death, and resurrection of His Son, Jesus Christ.

Can you imagine Noah, having seen no body of water larger than a river, adjusting to nautical life? He dealt with the change because he had a God-given mission. He took on a new vocation because God wanted him to provide a means for a better world.

Imagine the change Jesus experienced when he left His heavenly home to take up temporary residence on a corrupt planet that had once been His Father's masterpiece of perfect creation. He made the change for you. He changed you from sinner to saint. Just remember, that change is a work in progress! Someday, you'll be changing your residence too. You're bound to like Jesus' neighborhood.

Yes, change changes things—but one thing need never change: Jesus' promise to be with you forever. As someone who likely is closer than you are to the next phase of forever, I pray that you live with the same future as I—the one of which the apostle Paul wrote, "Now to Him who is able to do far more abundantly than all that we ask or think, according to the power at work within us, to Him be glory in the church and in Christ Jesus throughout all generations, forever and ever. Amen" (Ephesians 3:20–21).

2

Adjusting to a New World

Numbers 13–14

While the Israelites were wandering through the desert in search of a new homeland, they came across a place called Canaan, a land that "flows with milk and honey" (Numbers 13:27). The Israelites had been wandering in the desert for some time now, so a land flowing with milk and honey had to sound pretty amazing. The plunder the spies brought back had to seem pretty good—fresh fruit! More specifically, the kind needed to make wine! But rather than rally the people and use their excitement about the land's potential to overtake Canaan, all but two of the spies share their doubts. That becomes the Israelites' demise.

The doubters assemble the people and strongly suggest going back to Egypt. Perhaps they had already consumed some wine and forgotten the years of slavery and torment! Joshua and Caleb, the two spies who trusted God, were almost stoned for saying, "If the Lord delights in us, He will bring us into this land and give it to us" (Numbers 14:8). God saves Joshua and Caleb. In fact, they are the only two spies admitted to the Promised Land.

Starting a life in a new area can be exciting. It can also be overwhelming. My first move out of college was to central Illinois. I had grown up and gone to college in Chicagoland, and everything was within thirty minutes of one another. I really had no idea what it was like to live in a place that was not a suburb of a major city. To me, cities are "lands flowing with milk and honey." Everything you need is only a twenty- to thirty-minute drive away—and that's with traffic.

Central Illinois was a completely different world. Surrounded by corn or soybean fields, the cities and towns are very secluded—very much like bubbles. If the specific restaurant or store that you want is not in town, odds are you need to drive a good hour to the next big city, which I did on many occasions just to get my Chipotle fix!

The adjustment to central Illinois was very difficult for me. Almost immediately I was asked (remember we are still in Illinois), "Are you a Cubs fan or a Cards fan?" Being a diehard White Sox fan, I gave the appropriate response: "I'm a fan of the Sox and whoever is playing the Cubs!" I could not understand though—still being in Illinois—why there are no White Sox fans down here. The answer was made clear as soon as I tried to find the Sox television broadcast a few days later. I was in Cardinals territory!

Another tough adjustment moving away from my homeland was meeting people and finding things to do (more about that later). Growing up and going to college in the same area allowed me to continue seeing some of the same friends I had in grade school and high school. Now, I felt like I was on an island, even though I was only three hours from home. From my isolation came feelings very similar to those of the ten spies—overwhelmed, panicked, and hopeless.

God used those thoughts to help develop a stronger trust in Him. So many times we question God and what He is doing in our lives. So many times we say, "No! My way is much better!" Our plans end up like those of the Israelites who marched into the land of Canaan without the Lord and were destroyed. Why do we struggle against what God brings into our lives? Why do we argue the right path? Oftentimes, we even blame God for the consequences of our bad choices or decisions that did not demonstrate a trust in Him as our Provider. Perhaps the lesson to learn here is to trust God as our Guide—wherever we are!

I did not have much leadership in central Illinois. I learned a lot of things about my town and surrounding towns on my own, or from the youth I was serving. On my second move, to Southwest Michigan—a land flowing with craft beer and apples, the first item I received was a city map with important stores and restaurant locations. Rather than finding my own way around, the map made it much easier.

I love maps! Before many of my trips, I either purchase a map of my destination or I go online and check out a virtual map. I have often found that my GPS leads me to less-than-ideal locations while maps themselves are pretty accurate. For the most part, you can trust what you see on a map. Sometimes the scale interferes or the writing is too small, but maps are very trustworthy.

God has given you a map. It does not tell you exactly everything that is going to happen in your life, but it does tell you your destination. God's Word describes the journey of man's existence. It tells of the need for a Savior, and it tells of His journey to the cross, for you. Most important, it tells you that Christ's journey won a destination for you—the Promised Land! In that destination you will spend eternity never feeling overwhelmed, afraid, or hopeless. You will spend eternity with Him! Let God be your Guide. May His Word and grace guide you to that land flowing with milk and honey.

Reflection

The changes in your life often cause others to experience change too, so you aren't the only one making adjustments. For example, Aaron's departure to fulfill his first calling in ministry affected his parents—Renee and me. We missed him. Gone were things like witnessing how he teased his sister, hearing about his latest exploits at the White Sox game with Bob, and sleeplessly waiting to hear his car door close late at night. Renee and I never longed for the day we would be empty nesters. We had to adjust. Now, we look forward to the time when we're all joined together when Jesus returns to take us home.

As you make adjustments, be sympathetic to those who love you because they must work to adjust too.

The Bible if full of adjusters! When Judas adjusted to greed and unbelief, he left the other eleven of his group in crisis. Not only had he betrayed their trust—to say nothing of his Savior—but he also had left them to take on his previous duties. With God's help, they adjusted—though you might guess they never stopped mourning his loss.

With Jesus' closest followers often being slow to understand His teachings and actions, with the organized church plotting His demise, with sinners then and now—including you and me—continuing to live in sin, you might think Jesus would have made some adjustments in His sacrifice to save sinners. Why, in God's name, would He suffer and die to save those of fragile faith and weak commitment?

Why in God's name? That's it. God's name. Jesus obeyed the Father's will. He saved you in God's name. He knows your adjustment to being a saved sinner will not be perfect until you live with Him in heaven. He accepts repentance—as often as you repent; even then, he waits with open arms to welcome you back into His family. He promises not to adjust His forgiveness unless you yourself reject it.

In light of all the adjustments you'll be making—and causing, take comfort in knowing that Jesus will not adjust His love for you. Take this assurance: "But God shows His love for us in that while we were still sinners, Christ died for us" (Romans 5:8).

3

Bargain Hunting
Luke 16

I am a bargain hunter. I once bought two dress shirts, a tie, and a pair of shorts for a grand total of $14.38—total savings in the ballpark of $150. I always look for restaurant coupons or eat at restaurants on the days of a special that they are having. Around my birthday, I like to hit up all those places that give out freebies. For one birthday, I received coupons for a free mocha, a free cup of coffee with a pastry, a couple of free value meals, and half-price for a box of a dozen donuts. I like to think I am thrifty. My wife thinks I am cheap. Whichever way the coin falls, I find enjoyment in saving money on the items I buy.

The difference between the words *bargain* and *cheap* are extraordinary. While the word *bargain* denotes something of value for a less-than-expected cost, the word *cheap* indicates a lack of value or a loss of value completely. Money is a driving force of what we eat, what activities we do, and how we entertain. A lack of money can be even more influential in our financial decision-making. Ecclesiastes 5:10 says, "He who loves money will not be satisfied with money, nor he who loves wealth with his income; this also is vanity." Money will never be able to satisfy us. As creatures of the fall, we will always be yearning for something. We will always feel incomplete; money cannot fill the emptiness.

What would you do if you won a million dollars? Odds are you would upgrade your living conditions, get a new car, invest or put some money in the bank, travel, or possibly pay off some student loans. Some might donate to charities or help out family members. The hard part about winning money is that others also have expectations of what you'll do with your new wealth. If your sibling or parent won the money, would you expect to receive a share? Relationships and money tend to cause problems when they mix.

In 2012, about six months after our wedding, Andie and I decided to buy a house in Illinois. We were very excited, had been approved for a loan, and signed the contract. A few days later, I received a call to southwest Michigan. We talked to the bank and our realtor and thought we could get out of the deal, but the sellers were not under the same impression. After a few discussions with lawyers and other professionals in the real estate field, it was determined that if the matter was taken to court, a judge could rule in favor of either one of us.

During that process, Andie had turned in her two-week notice. As a result, the bank said they could no longer approve us for a loan. We thought we were off the hook! Apparently, that did not help our case either. We were stuck with a house we had to buy without a bank loan to buy it! That is when my parents got involved. They offered to loan us the money so we could buy the house and hopefully sell it quickly.

There was no hesitation in accepting their offer. The relationship of parent to child was stronger than figuring out all the details involving money. I admire and respect my parents for their assistance. They could have easily let us figure it out on our own. There was a mutual understanding of the sacrifice it took in order for this to happen as well.

In the three long years following this event, no one expected the roller coaster ride that ensued. But during those three years of making payments and figuring out our own finances, my parents never once made us feel bad about the sacrifice they made. That was a valued part of the relationship which already existed. There was a mutual effort put into the relationship. We worked hard to do our part, and they worked hard to be patient and understanding.

You may have heard the saying "Don't do business with family." It can be true. (That is another life lesson.) My parents taught me that family is there for one another. They also taught me to not be so attached to money that I could not let it go, but to also not be so frivolous and irresponsible with money that I did not have enough to take care of myself.

In Luke 16:10–13, Jesus talks about money, saying:

> One who is faithful in a very little is also faithful in much, and one who is dishonest in a very little is also dishonest in much. If then you have not been faithful in the unrighteous wealth, who will entrust to you the true riches? And if you have not been faithful in that which is another's, who will give you that which is your own? No servant can serve two masters, for either he will hate the one and love the other, or he will be devoted to the one and despise the other. You cannot serve God and money. We will be looking at different parts of this Scripture in future chapters, but for now let's focus on serving two masters. It is hard to overcome serving money, but when you give freely to God what you have been given, you are no longer a prisoner to the lure of money. When you obey God's command to love others no matter what the cost, the cost doesn't seem so great.

Jesus paid the price so you could have a relationship with God once again. It was not cheap. He paid the price of His own blood. On the cross, He suffered hours of torment and pain, abandonment, and false accusations. Ultimately, He paid with His life.

The free gift of grace you receive is priceless! God's grace allows you to rely on Him completely. When you serve God rather than self or money, you allow Him to use you to guide others into relationship with Him. God loves you and wants you to be responsible with what He's given you. Let Him use you to help free others from financial bondage.

Reflection

When Aaron first called us, our initial reaction went something like this: Gulp! You bought a house?! Great, your Illinois apartment was too small anyway.

Gulp, gulp!! You're moving to Michigan to continue your ministry, and Andie will find a job there? Great!

Gulp, gulp, gulp!!! You have to buy the house in Illinois—the one you can't live in and have no means of paying for it?! Gulp to end all gulps!

Even with an occasional gulp or two, we'll figure out a way to address the problem. Your lives are important to us. Your new ministry will provide new ways to bless others through the blessings God has given you. God is helping us through all that right now. Even with an occasional gulp or two.

Money creates problems, and money solves problems. Many people spend their entire lives worrying about how to spend money or how to find ways to make more spending possible. And some spend on savings and investments, all of which have proven risky at times.

Money and finances are major causes of anxiety and relationship difficulties. You can understand why the Bible addressed money. Finances were at the heart of the feud between Jacob and Esau (Genesis 25–35), the betrayal of Jesus (Matthew 26), and the deaths of Ananias and Sapphira (Acts 5).

Money never saves with any eternal consequences. Only Jesus saves, as we see in the meaning of the second article of the Apostles' Creed:

> Jesus Christ . . . has redeemed me . . . purchased and won me from all sins, from death, and from the power of the devil; not with gold or silver, but with His holy, precious blood and with His innocent suffering and death, that I may be His own. (Small Catechism, Second Article)

You are indeed His own. Gulp!

4

Talking to Yourself

1 Thessalonians 5:16–18

Okay, be honest. How often do you find yourself having a dialogue with no one else in the room?

One recent grad I spoke with mentioned she talks to her frying pan. Whether you monologue (or is it dialogue?) with yourself or an inanimate object, keep in mind that the behavior is pretty typical when no one else is around. In public, that's a different story.

One time, I was standing in the grocery store next to someone who was trying to pick out a cereal, and he started talking. I answered his question as best I could before realizing he was talking on a hands-free device. Too proud to laugh it off with the stranger, I quickly grabbed whatever box was in front of me and scurried off.

In public, talking to yourself can drive others to steer clear—which you may choose to do in rush-hour traffic just to clear a path. In private, it is normal to want to hear some noise or to clarify your thoughts out loud, just to keep your sanity. (By the way, this is a great reason to get a dog!)

If you are by yourself, then you are at an amazing, special, and unique time in your life. You might feel alone, lame, and desperate for friendship or a social life. Take a lesson from the first letter to the Thessalonians:

"Rejoice always, pray without ceasing, give thanks in all circumstances" (5:16). Sounds like a party for one!

For what can you be joyful at this time in your life? For what can you give thanks? This is a great time to reflect on the wonderful blessings God gives you. It is also a great time to work on your relationship with Him.

God is present in your life. You may not see it very clearly, or you might be unaware as to how to see God's presence. You are not alone!

Elijah, after killing the prophets of Baal, fled for his life. He ran to a mountain in the wilderness. As the Word of the Lord came to him, Elijah sought out God's presence. At first, there was a mighty, rushing wind, but God was not in the wind. Next, came an earthquake. But God was not in the earthquake. After the earthquake there was a fire—and while God had used fire before with Moses and the burning bush, God was not in the fire. Do you remember how Elijah sees the presence of God? In a whisper—a gentle, quiet breath (1 Kings 19:9–18).

Think about the last time someone whispered to you. Did you have to listen harder? Stay focused? Pay attention? Hearing a whisper requires the listener to get rid of all distraction and noise and quiet any inner voices that might drown out the speaker. Perhaps to see God's presence a little clearer, you will have to quiet yourself and devote your attention to Him.

I learned a good lesson in tuning in to God's presence on a servant event in North Carolina. Cell phone reception was spotty at best in the mountains, and our camp and worksite were in dead zones. Each day, we would drive through the town of Boone, and my phone would buzz for a good minute or two while catching up on texts, emails, and missed calls from the night before. However, I was driving, so I was powerless to respond. That was a true lesson in listening!

I began to appreciate areas of reception, though I do admit it was nice to be out of reach with the rest of the world for a few days. That experience made me think about my reception with God. Am I at five bars, eager and open to receiving His messages? Or am I in a dead zone, not even trying to find a signal? In Paul's terms, am I praying unceasingly or just every now and then?

When you're in an area of "good reception," it is easier to see God's presence and to value your relationship with Him. You can improve your reception by being in the Word daily, rejoicing and trusting in Him in all circumstances, appreciating what He is doing in your life, and serving those around you. When you see God's presence in your life, it is much easier to trust Him in times of trial and loneliness. Elijah was empowered by God's presence to keep going.

Talk to God. Take time to grow closer to Him and to develop a stronger relationship with Him. Look for those times when He clearly says, "I love you; you are mine!" Work on getting better reception. I encourage you to pray unceasingly, continually, and to stop talking to yourself!

Reflection

Do you talk to yourself? In my younger years, if it seemed that you were talking to yourself, you really were talking to yourself. If caught in the act, you would have been thankful for a hands-free device. Talk about being embarrassed! Older people would snicker about the lad they saw talking to Cap'n Crunch! Of course, you could always fight back by putting the box to your ear and saying something like, "Yeah, that old guy was making fun of me." Not that I know anyone who would do such a thing.

Talking to yourself may lead to self-deception too. When nobody listens to what you have to say, talking to yourself provides at least one engaged listener. Yet, there always is a risk that you do not understand what you are talking about any more than anyone else.

Talking to God is a good alternative to talking to yourself, though it is not entirely risk free. Poor, childless Hannah was mistakenly thought to be drunk in church because the passionate prayer on her lips could not be heard (1 Samuel 1:13).

Listening to God—especially His whisper, as Aaron mentioned—may pose some unexpected experiences too, on par with talking to yourself.

Hearing voices can be handled with medication, but some believers think that that is how you listen to God. Often, they are disappointed when they don't hear personally from the Maker. Sometimes they do hear voices, but they are devilish delusions, not divine revelation.

God speaks to you through the Bible. Believers need to be in the Word, listening to it instead of talking to themselves.

Try this: Find a good Bible. You don't even need to spend lots of money; search the Web for reliable, free Bible resources such as www.biblegateway.com.

You will find that the Bible has something godly to say for every issue that has you talking to yourself.

5

CONSEQUENCES
Genesis 3

By now you must realize that the "real world" is different from the bubble you experienced in college. Whether you studied through an online program, at a community college, a smaller private college, or a larger state university, you have been somewhat sheltered and protected from the real world simply because of your age. Now don't get mad and quit reading this chapter—age has been a qualifier since Paul's day: "Let no one despise you for your youth, but set the believers an example in speech, in conduct, in love, in faith, in purity" (1 Timothy 4:12).

Your first year out of college in the "real world" probably consists of "grown-up things"— things like finding a health insurance plan, working on a budget, learning to cook, finding your own way around town, setting up an apartment or house, finding a church home, taking a day of vacation to wait for the cable guy, and all other responsibilities that show maturity. All of a sudden, the world isn't such a carefree place anymore!

You might learn the hard way the consequences of being late to an interview versus being late for class. The real world has real consequences—consequences that might have been less severe in college. Adam and Eve learned first-hand about this truth. They were given a garden of perfection—a bubble, if you want to think about it that way. Outside influences were not a factor. God gave them everything they needed. But then they disobeyed. Enter consequences. Guilt, shame, and blame all start to corrupt their relationships. Welcome to the real world, Adam and Eve!

It must have been pretty scary leaving the garden. No more late-morning walks with God. No more low-maintenance crops. Unusual feelings such as sadness, jealousy, and inadequacy now plague their emotions. Are you feeling some of those same emotions? Are you having a hard time adjusting to feelings you haven't had before?

I remember moving into my first apartment. It was exciting to finally be living on my own. I was not accountable to anyone, I could cook what I wanted, I didn't have to wash the dishes until I wanted to, and, within reason, I could do anything I wanted. Sounds pretty selfish. But the excitement of independence quickly faded after I was all moved in and my family left—I was all alone.

I couldn't even sleep in my bed that first night. I finally managed to catch a few hours of sleep on the futon while watching a movie. My first night "out of the bubble" was rough. Not only was I leaving the bubble of college, I was also leaving the bubble of my family and friends—the only life I had known. After that first night, I started to develop a routine, and life as I knew it took on a different form.

I learned back in grade school that consequences can be good and bad. Praise God that He did not just leave the negative consequences to destroy the world after Adam and Eve. A promise also came as a result of the fall. The Savior of the world would come. Did Adam and Eve still have to deal with real-world consequences? Definitely! Will you still have to deal with real-world consequences? Yes, sin makes sure of that! But you do not have to face these consequences as if there was no hope. "Christ Jesus came into the world to save sinners" (1 Timothy 1:15).

Christ's sacrifice was the solution to the consequence of sin. It is the entire reason He came! Because of His death and resurrection, you receive His grace. What a great consequence! What a great blessing! "See what kind of love the Father has given to us, that we should be called children of God" (1 John 3:1).

The lesson here? No matter the consequence you are enduring—positive or negative—live in God's grace and fully rely on Him.

Reflection

Some consequences are a long time coming.

I smoked heavily for ten years. Stopping was tortuous. The nicotine addiction seemed innocuous. Attempts to quit smoking wrestled with years of habit. The fight was bitter, and temptations persisted even years after victory.

Delayed consequences make me think of an oil filter commercial. A mechanic holding a dripping oil filter intones, "You can pay me now, or you can pay me later."

The Ten Commandments provide another good example. They are easy to break and even easier to ignore. The consequences often seem, well, inconsequential. For those who think the Ten Commandments apply only to those who actually believe in God, the consequences of breaking them seem all but invisible.

A close look at the Commandments, combined with some not-so-deep thinking, reveals the astounding news that these ten laws are God's provision for happiness. Imagine the quality of life if only people could—and wanted to—obey these ancient but timeless rules.

Old, irrelevant laws? No personal consequences? It's not rocket science to perceive how life is stained, if not outright ruined, by the consequences of sin.

Look at your life. Look at your relationships—even the best of them. Imperfections taint all relationships, and eventually death will break them. Death—the ultimate consequence of a sin-infiltrated life.

These are the consequences of sin that led to Jesus' consequences in ancient times, in my time, in your time. It's almost enough to make you bitter, pessimistic, and plagued by the shadows of dread.

Almost.

From the very first sin, God held out hope. Before Adam and Eve were even evicted, God promised a Savior who would crush Satan's head and defeat his power. God's promise persisted through centuries of His people's cycles of tragedies and triumphs.

You are among His people today! Sinners? Absolutely. Forgiven sinners? Absolutely, absolutely. And there is more:

But God, being rich in mercy, because of the great love with which He loved us, even when we were dead in our trespasses, made us alive together with Christ . . . For by grace you have been saved through faith. And this is not your own doing; it is the gift of God, not a result of works, so that no one may boast. For we are His workmanship, created in Christ Jesus for good works, which God prepared beforehand, that we should walk in them. (Ephesians 2:4–5, 8–10)

6

End Results

Romans 8:28

Did you "know that for those who love God all things work together for good" (Romans 8:28)? In the midst of life's chaos and problems, it can be hard to connect the dots and see the silver linings.

Sometimes a situation is just terrible, and there is no good that comes from the bad things that are happening. But don't lose faith! I am sure you have heard a hundred stories of bad situations turned good. Well, sit back and listen to one hundred and one!

I received a call to serve as Director of Christian Education at a small congregation in central Illinois. The town in which I served had quite a few churches, including multiple congregations of my denomination. When the recession of 2008 trickled down and impacted our congregation, money became tight. Already struggling in my relationships with my pastor and a few leaders in the congregation, I knew the financial problems just made the whole situation worse.

One day, the congregation president, along with the head elder, came in to have a discussion with me. No decisions had been made, but I was warned that if the financial situation didn't improve, my job could be reduced to part-time. All my thoughts turned to how I could survive on half of my church worker's salary. I would have to move to a smaller apartment, possibly get a roommate, learn to live on ramen noodles, and give up my addiction to Culvers. I unhappily left the discussion and started to search for jobs. Interestingly enough, a theology degree doesn't present many opportunities to work outside of the Church.

The leadership and pastor at my church worked hard to find another way to keep me at full-time. Their efforts resulted in a split position with another congregation in town. I would be teaching Confirmation classes at the Christian day school more regularly, as well as lead chapel at the nursing home.

Really? Nursing home chapels? I was not excited and pretty upset with the agreement, but it meant that I would be a full-time employee and would not have to change vocations.

The first day of chapel at the nursing home was exhausting and draining. The emotional toll of seeing people in distress was too much. I prayed. I pleaded with God to let there be another way! But the answer was clear. I would be leading chapel for a while.

Chapels started to get better. I developed relationships with the awesome volunteers and also with many of the residents. The messages I delivered became easier to write and helped me reflect on my own life as I shared stories and experiences that were evidence of God at work. This ministry that I did not think I would be able to survive became a blessing! The faithful volunteers who so joyfully shared God's love became a main reason why I stayed in ministry during that trying time.

I share that story because sometimes life seems to be headed in a direction you don't want to take. Oftentimes, major decisions need to be made that really have no positive outlook any way you look at it. But I encourage you to trust in God.

I doubted. I failed to submit to God's will and tried to fight it. I have gotten a lot better at trusting God. Deuteronomy 29:29 says, "The secret things belong to the Lord our God, but the things that are revealed belong to us and to our children forever, that we may do all the words of this law."

I read through this verse a couple times, but it never really had any meaning to me—I mean come on, Deuteronomy? But "all Scripture is breathed out by God and profitable" (2 Timothy 3:16).

I love the connection this verse has to Romans 8:28. There are actually things we are not meant to know. If you learn accept this, then you learn to trust God even in times that do not make sense. God reveals some things to us throughout all of Scripture. But other things remain secret—we may not understand why something is happening. A college professor once taught me that the answer to the question, "Why do bad things happen to good people?" should be "I don't know; it's okay to not know."

God loves you. He wants you to live in His grace, His glory, and His way. He gives you the Law—the right way of living. More important, He also gives you grace—the free gift of undeserved love.

God is not against you. A positive attitude is important to seeing the good in bad situations. When bad things are happening or you are in the middle of a situation you don't understand, I hope you develop an attitude of humility and grace, of patience and maturity. Learning to live in the love He promises and so graciously gives you!

Reflection

I remember when Aaron told me about his visit with his congregation's leaders. After years of professional church work myself, my sage advice unfortunately went something like this: "Get out of there! Run!"

With my integrity and wisdom from experience temporarily out of order, passion and anger took over. Flee! Leave small-town Illinois in the same dust that so rapidly accumulated from decaying manufacturers, once powerful and profitable but now in economic trauma.

Chances are good that you, too, will face occupational hazards, not the least of which will be unemployment. Perhaps you're even starting out that way, without the privilege of having a job to lose. Whatever will be the end results?

You may need to move back home, if that's a possibility. You may need to work at something for which you are unprepared and unmotivated. Perhaps you fear homelessness. You are almost sure to wonder where God is in all this, especially when you are reading a religious book like this.

Flexibility is the key to dealing with end results—and influencing them. Blaming God—or suspecting His apathy—is not an option. After all, consider His words through Jeremiah during one of Jeremiah's low points in life. Scripture says, "For I know the plans I have for you, declares the LORD, plans for welfare and not for evil, to give you a future and a hope" (Jeremiah 29:11).

Run. Run even when you don't need to. Run to God in prayer and worship and study. He knows your end result. So do you. The only thing you do not know is all that will happen in between. It is okay not to know. Sometimes the only thing you can do is trust God. Truth be told, it is the only thing you can ever do.

7

Waiting on Tables

Mark 10:45

Have you noticed how rude people can be toward the wait staff at a restaurant? Maybe you have been a waiter or waitress. Servers truly are servants. They are tasked with making sure you have all the amenities you need, as well as to wait on you hand and foot. Good waiters and waitresses know how to be unobtrusive, anticipate needs, and make personal connections with those whom they serve. When the customer is not happy or treats them as a servant, the wait staff needs to exercise humility to the max!

Servers are frequently not fully appreciated. Their work often goes unnoticed. Do you remember the name of the person who last served you food? Unless you have served, you cannot truly appreciate those who serve.

The same is true in serving others in life. Consider the similarities between food servers and God's servants. You typically do not get to choose whom you serve. You might be asked to serve the most annoying, rude, and unappreciative person in the world. You might be asked to serve a friend. You might even be led to serve an ordinary person whose impact on you is minimal at most. But all service experiences demonstrate the importance of your love for God and your neighbor.

I've worked on and led a number of servant events in various parts of the United States. Some lasted a few hours, others a week or more. One of my most memorable service experiences was in New Orleans in 2006.

Nine months after Katrina hit, the city was still in dire need. Abandoned properties, piles of junk, and an air of hopelessness besieged the city, and I certainly would not have chosen to serve the homeowner we were assigned. He was a washed-out rock star who drank beer while he worked on his house. All judgments aside, beer just isn't the best beverage choice when working in a hazmat suit in 98-degree weather with 100 percent humidity!

It was difficult cleaning out this man's house because he didn't want to throw away any of his memories. I can't blame him. As we served this man and helped restore hope in the community, the Holy Spirit took over! This man—who at the beginning of the week was skeptical that one twenty-year-old guy, four college girls, and an elderly couple could actually help him—was so moved by all our hard work and accomplishments that he wanted to know more about Christ. He wanted to know more about why this eclectic group would give up a week of their summer to help out a complete stranger. The Holy Spirit moved him to faith, and this man became a believer!

While this servant event had a dramatic conclusion, not every trip works out that way. On another trip to New Orleans, my group was assigned to serve a lady who needed some help with putting the finishing touches on her house. We did a lot of detail work for her, all of which never seemed good enough. Meanwhile, her able-bodied son sat and watched television while we sweated in the heat. My attitude of a willing servant quickly turned sour. It was hard to see the need for or the value of our work.

Servants are called to do the dirty work. They are called to wash feet. They are called to clean toilets and be patient with rude people. Being a servant is not an easy job! Colossians 3:23–34 reminds us, "Whatever you do, work heartily, as for the Lord and not for men, knowing that from the Lord you will receive the inheritance as your reward. You are serving the Lord Christ."

Even when your service seems unappreciated or under-valued, remember you are serving God. Through your service, you will be able to identify with people and make connections with those serving alongside you. The best servants act just like the best restaurant servers: unobtrusive, able to anticipate the needs of others, and able to make personal connections with those they serve.

As a child of God, you are called to serve. Where you serve may not be in a far-away city on a servant event or even in the context of your church family. But all service teaches humility—an important quality that is not very prevalent in the world. Humility reminds us that we need a Savior and that we cannot make it to heaven on our own. Service also teaches us to love—to put the needs of others before ourselves. Even Jesus came to serve, not to be served (Mark 10:45).

As you begin to develop your own routine, be sure to include time to serve others. You may have a lot of needs yourself, but by keeping others' needs in mind, it helps you keep God first in your life. Be a reflection of His love to those around you!

Reflection

Servers sometimes have trouble accepting service. They grow accustomed to being on the giving end, where they feel competent, skilled, and confident. Servers can even become grumpy and grudging, feeling as if they need help from no one. Sometimes unthankful for it too.

Perhaps you already have an attitude of gratitude toward those who do things for you. If not, it might be time to develop one. It will make you a better person now, and it will become a necessity as you age.

Here is a less-than-dramatic example: When Aaron was first learning to fish, I needed to tie the fisherman's knots for his snap swivel or lure. The knots were complicated (for me), and I was proud of myself for demonstrating the perfect knot—at least until it unraveled under duress! Now, my fishing partner—usually Renee these days—ties my knots. Oh, I start them, but it does not take long for frustration to set in, and rescue is at hand. I say "thank you," but I utter it reluctantly.

God's people can be reluctant to accept help also. It happens because human nature wants to be in charge—to be successful. But that attitude can be dangerous.

You must guard against thinking that you can help yourself to heaven. You may think participating in servant events or going to church or contributing to charities are ways to "help your cause." Oh, you thank God for sending Jesus to be your Savior, but surely there are things you can—or need to—do to help.

Wrong!

Everything needed to take away your sins and earn eternal life in heaven has been done for you. Jesus Christ is the ultimate Servant. His life, death, and resurrection come compliments of God the Father, who loves you—even when you get a little grumpy or grudging with gratitude.

Paul says, "For by grace you have been saved through faith. And this is not your own doing; it is the gift of God, not a result of works, so that no one may boast" (Ephesians 2:8–9).

And about your service to others, Paul adds this in verse 10: "For we are His workmanship, created in Christ Jesus for good works, which God prepared beforehand, that we should walk in them."

8

Freshman Fifteen

1 Corinthians 6:19–20

Welcome to your freshman year . . . after college. (Unless you're a grad student; in that case, welcome to your freshman year!) During your freshman year of college, you are expected to gain fifteen pounds, commonly referred to as the "Freshman Fifteen." This is probably due to the freedom surrounding your diet, as well as a lack of exercise corresponding to sports. But I am not sure I met too many people who gained that much weight their first year. I certainly did not!

During my stint in college, I was really active. I played on the tennis team, and between off-season conditioning and in-season training, I found myself burning calories as fast as I consumed them—which was good because my friends and I had more of an appetite for late-night Wendy's and Arby's runs than healthy cafeteria food. Plus, long walks on campus—especially in winter in the wind tunnel from the parking garage to my dorm—really forced me to stay active. I also played on intramural teams and ran around the community in the evenings and on weekends. When I think back, rarely was I sedentary.

But then graduation happens. Now what? Instead of walking to class, you sit at a desk. In place of Ultimate Frisbee, there is binge-watching seasons of your favorite television shows on Netflix. Instead of hitting up the salad bar at the cafeteria, it is much easier to stop by KFC for some fried chicken.

For me, my first year in the work force was rough on my physical fitness. I tried running, biking, and rollerblading, but I only went as far as the mailbox down the street, a mile round trip. I received a free, three-month membership at the YMCA but could not afford to maintain a membership afterward. I thought about biking to work, but the five-mile stretch had few safe routes. I found myself eating healthier foods, but I really missed the regular exercise.

I have been pretty active my whole life—shooting hoops in the driveway, playing tennis in high school with my sister or friends, tossing around a baseball with my dad after he got home from work—but that first year out of college was tough!

A large part of staying physically fit is a positive attitude. The words of 1 Corinthians 6:19–20 played a large part in helping me stay in shape, both physically and spiritually. Paul writes: "Or do you not know that your body is a temple of the Holy Spirit within you, whom you have from God? You are not your own, for you were bought with a price. So glorify God in your body."

The things going into your body and mind directly affect what comes out. If you are eating unhealthy food, it will affect your overall health. Likewise, if your mind is taking in junk, your actions and attitude suffer.

What are you consuming? Are you getting your full nutrition from God's Word and in prayer? Or are you hitting up the drive-thru and filling up on quick-fixes with no sustenance?

During this "freshman" year of your life, I encourage you to gain that fifteen—not in the physical sense but in your walk with God. Take fifteen minutes in the morning and at night to work on your temple—your body, your heart, your mind, your soul. Get it in shape both physically and spiritually. When you are spiritually healthy, it is much easier to be a reflection of that amazing love that Jesus won for you on the cross!

Reflection

Survive the threat to your personal well-being! Make it past the first "fifteen," and you are in store for another. Just think about the senior (as in age fifty-five plus) one hundred.

You may think it unimaginable, but it takes little effort to gain one hundred pounds after college graduation. All you need is puny willpower, diminutive self-discipline, and some old college intramural injury that obstructs a serious fitness routine!

Pizza, hot dogs, craft beer, fund-raiser candy sales, and a myriad of other mass-produced and mouth-watering foods aside, obesity is a contemporary and pervasive problem. It is not something to take lightly . . . or even to pun about. There is one exception, and Aaron suggested it.

Be a spiritual heavyweight. Here is a sample diet:

Consume a lot of God's Word. It comes in several flavors. First, munch away on the Bible. You have a choice of many versions via various websites. Compare what you read in one version with what you read in another. Enjoy the flavors!

Dine with a group. Pass along the Word in group Bible study. Most congregations have at least one. You will not find everything on this menu to your liking. Some studies may be a bit bland and some too heavy. Explore the buffet until you find one that will help you grow. If your church doesn't have a group, consider starting one.

Stick it in your ear. While this is not considered acceptable beyond infancy when it comes to food, it is a Bible-recommended way of feasting on Scripture (Luke 11:28). Hear the Word of God by attending worship services. Regardless of how it is prepared or delivered, be assured that Scripture always nourishes—sometimes many years after first ingested. The Holy Spirit works through the Word, regardless of how it is consumed. Through the Word, the Spirit nourishes faith.

Snack on prayer. Experienced snackers need little reason to indulge. The same is true for those who pray. Pray for every little reason. You don't need to wait for some big reason to come along. God is interested in all areas of your life. You don't even need to ask for anything. Are you enjoying a bracing morning? Bless the Lord for giving you cool breezes and pleasant weather to enjoy. Did you make a new friend? Thank God for friendships.

Prayer comes in several flavors too:

Ready-made prayers. Martin Luther wrote a few dandies in his Morning and Evening Prayers. (If you don't know them, I encourage you to look them up online.) Of course, the Lord's Prayer is most people's favorite.

Prayers you make up. Back when Aaron was in junior-high confirmation class, I asked his class if they used any books of prayer or if they would like to have one. Nearly all said no. This was disheartening, especially because I was working on a prayer book at the time! It was not that they did not pray; they were comfortable making up their own. You can be comfortable too.

Give meals to others who are hungry. Pray for others. You may even find out that God has given you answers to your own prayers!

I pray that you enjoy your new freedoms and responsibilities. I pray that you see God in all of them. And just as Aaron sometimes confers with me about decisions or ideas, feel free to confer with your Father. He wants to hear from you. He even wrote a Book for you.

9

Hot-Button Issues

Psalm 46

How do you feel about politics? Are you a Democrat, Republican, or Independent? Think about the judgments you just made when reading those words.

Society seems to think that if you don't express a stance on abortion or gender issues, then you must not be staying current with what's going on in the world. No matter the current world issue, everyone seems to have an opinion. Thanks to social media, it seems everyone's opinions are valid and matter greatly. When scrolling down my profile page, it is like a thousand little voices all speaking at once! (Okay, you caught me, I don't have near that number of friends.) Even the thirty or forty voices I hear every day produce a mind-numbing cacophony. How did the world ever survive before social media?

More and more I am seeing and realizing that, as Christians, we are in exile. To speak out against abortion is seen as judgmental and chauvinistic. To say aloud that God instituted marriage to be between one man and one woman is an invitation for others to call you close-minded and hateful. Are you afraid to express your opinions and beliefs? Maybe the tougher question should be, "What are your opinions based upon?"

As Christians, we are called be God's representatives in this place (2 Corinthians 5:20). In order to be good ambassadors, we have to have His facts straight! Those facts are clear in the Bible, but sometimes we need some help from those who have more theological training.

When discussions about hot-button issues occur, they frequently turn into arguments. Why? It probably has something to do with the term itself. Hot-button issues evoke a lot of emotion in people. Sometimes your views on certain subjects are shaped by secret reasons, personal life experiences, or family expectations. That is true for other people as well. It is important to remember that *you* represent God in the discussion!

Jesus did not shy away from hot-button issues. In fact, He hung out with the social outsiders and those in the midst of heated disputes on topics such as taxes, the government, religious laws, and sin. In Matthew 22:37–39, Jesus taught people two foundational rules for life: Love God; love others. How can you live out those principles the next time you engage in a discussion on a hot-button issue? How can you live out these principles while voicing your opinions on certain divisive issues?

Since you are an exile in this world, society will always seem to go against your opinions founded in Scripture. The world always tries to twist the Word of God to accommodate what it wants you to believe. It is an uphill battle. But take heart! Read more about God, our Fortress, in Psalm 46.

When I was younger, my sister and I would sometimes play American Gladiators. We would set up chairs as our stations and place different Nerf guns at each post. The goal was to hit a target above the gladiator's head before your opponent hit you. The start of the course had the most protective chairs, the ones with mesh between the rungs. As we got closer and closer to each other—opposing gladiators—the chairs became more sparse and less protective. Our mini fortresses had flaws, but they still required enemy arrows to be accurate and on target.

With God as your fortress, there are no weak spots in His protection. You become vulnerable when you walk outside of His love and care and try to make it on your own. How great to read the first verse of Psalm 46 and understand that even when we try and fail on our own, "God is our refuge and strength, a very present help in trouble." He is there, wanting us to come back under His protection.

I love verse 10 too. "Be still," it begins. So when all the voices of society pull you in different directions and create chaos, remember that God commands you to be still.

When I envision being still, my mind imagines a winter night. It's well after dark, and I'm shoveling the driveway as snow still gently falls. No one is around, and the snow blankets the world in silence. A quick pause in my work and the silence envelopes me. That is how I envision God's stillness. There is peace, there is quiet, and there is comfort. All other thoughts fade away. If the world is sounding a little chaotic, it might be time to unplug. It might be time to take a vacation or seek out a silent place.

In God's protection, silence abounds. No matter the hot-button issue, take comfort in knowing God is there and that He loves you. Focus on how to best love Him by loving others and being an agent of the Gospel. Most important, live in His forgiveness and trust in His promise to be your fortress.

Reflection

What's this about American Gladiators? I can see Aaron in combat against some imaginary army, but his sister? Allison? Peace-loving, sweet, obedient, and kind Allison? Nary a hint of battle remained whenever we returned home. However, this could account for a few inexplicable nicks in the furniture.

You are indeed going to need your fortresses, as Aaron explained. The world is becoming more unfriendly—even intolerant—to Christians like you.

When Allison and Aaron were young, Renee and I enjoyed the innocence of their infancy and looked forward to observing their growth in mind, body, and faith. But at some point, those visions of "sugar plums" became shriveled prunes. Trepidation set in. World events shadowed hopes and joys. Our children would live in an increasingly wicked world.

You have or will have fears of the future when and if you have children. You will need a fortress not only for yourself but also for your family. You will need to add a few rooms onto your fortress.

How will you do that? As Aaron said, fortify yourself and your loved ones with Psalm 46. Do it early. Do it often. Invite others inside.

Many people avoid hot-button issues. Their fortresses are places to hide from the enemy. They cloister themselves away from the world rather than place a welcome mat at the gate. They refuse to speak out and stand up for issues and instead cower quietly inside their protective walls.

Thanks be to God; your fortress stands boldly and battered right out in the open. Your fortress will not spare you the scars of battle nor afford you the honor of a grateful society. Sin will never give up in trying to take you prisoner or kill you. You always will need the power of the Holy Spirit backing the truths of God's Word, which everyone so desperately needs to know.

Troubling thoughts, huh? The whole truth and nothing but the truth is a hot button itself. Put on your gloves! Okay, so you will need more than that in your fortresses closet . . . Try this:

> Therefore take up the whole armor of God, that you may be able to withstand in the evil day, and having done all, to stand firm. Stand therefore, having fastened on the belt of truth, and having put on the breastplate of righteousness, and, as shoes for your feet, having put on the readiness given by the gospel of peace. (Ephesians 6:13–15)

10

Finding Value in Your Job
Job 1

What did you want to be when you grew up?

Isn't it great? Living the dream! All the pieces fell into place, and there is no more room to rise. You set your own hours, have unlimited vacation days, and the boss takes you out for lunch at least once a week. Pay is a little less than you think you are worth, but six figures is a pretty good starting salary, right?

Yeah, right!

Most likely, you are not in this scenario. You may even be in quite the opposite situation!

In the Old Testament, Job seemed to have it all. The man had livestock aplenty, sons and daughters who seemingly got along pretty well, and land as far as the eye could see. Job was "the greatest of all the people of the east" (Job 1:3b).

But then Satan believed Job would turn away from God if Job was not so well off. Job's life started to take a tumble. His children tragically died, his land was invaded and taken away, and even his health took a turn for the worse. Talk about falling from grace!

Do you feel like you are in a time of plenty or a time of hardship? That question could be answered in many ways, not simply based on physical possessions. Are you finding your work meaningful? Do you feel part of your workplace community? Are you in a stopover position on your way to the top? Maybe you cannot even find a job! Life is a little more difficult than it seemed when you were growing up, isn't it?

My wife, Andie, has an interesting career story. She has been a hostess, a Certified Nurse Assistant at an assisted living center, a lab tech, a project manager, and she has worked in a pharmacy. She has always had at least two incomes due to side jobs involving tumbling or dance. She is a hard worker, but she has not yet reached her final destination. She's currently attending grad school to become a forensics specialist.

It has been quite a journey for Andie. Before she became a project manager, she was unhappy with her job. While some of the stress was due to the work itself, most of the stress came in the form of her coworkers. After a long deliberation, Andie decided to submit her two-week notice.

Being the practical person I am, I struggled with her decision. I knew how unhappy she was and how it was affecting her health and attitude, so I was supportive. But I wanted a contingency plan. We certainly were not in the land of plenty like Job at the beginning of his story, but I did not want to end up like Job in the middle either!

God was watching out for us though. Andie went to her boss to turn in her notice, but before she put the envelope on his desk, he offered her a new position. I can imagine her trying to hide the envelope any way possible as she said, "Go on . . ." The position was not necessarily a promotion, but it involved a significant pay increase and a different supervisor. The practical side of me was put to shame by my lack of trust in God.

It is interesting to read through the Book of Job and see where his success originated. God blessed Job with all that he had because Job was upright and blameless. He did what God told him to do. He trusted God. He found value and success in obedience to God's Word. He even watched out for his family by making offerings for them in case they had sinned. Here is a dad watching out for his children!

What a great example of how the Father watches out for you, His child. Romans 5:8 puts it into perspective: "God shows His love for us in that while we were still sinners, Christ died for us." Job's life was severely affected by sin in the world. Satan took full advantage of his agents and took everything from Job, except Job's three bothersome friends. But even with their constant chattering in Job's ear, he did not turn away from God.

Knowing the imperfection that is your life, take comfort in the power of the cross. The sacrifice was made on your behalf not *just in case* you mess up. We can trust God in all His promises. He is always faithful. Look at how Job ended up (Job 42:10–17). God blessed Job with twice what he had started with! No matter where you are right now in your journey of life, find value in knowing that you are God's beloved child.

Reflection

When I was a young child, I wanted to be a garbage man—that's what we in Chicago called the men who worked the alleys to pick up the trash. They had a huge orange truck. They yelled a lot and banged around the fifty-five-gallon steel drums holding the smelly trash. I wanted to be one of them mostly because they were the only ones I could see working from the window in the back flat of my building.

As it turned out, those garbage men made a lot more money than I did during the first few years I taught in a Christian school. I never really planned on teaching. But the Holy Spirit kept pushing me, mostly through less-than-successful school experiences until I landed at a small college that would take me. Even then I resisted. Yet the Spirit got in the way of my plans as a business major, a psychology major, and, well, I ended up graduating from another small Christian college with a degree in education. And it was the best thing ever . . . most of the time. But not always.

God doesn't always work things out to our contentment. You have heard, "All things work together for good, for those who are called according to His purpose" (Romans 8:28). His purpose for you may be hard to accept until you are blessed with enough age to have hindsight. But even hindsight is not an asset unless you are willing to see all that God has done through you in your vocation.

For example, my goals as a young adult (fifty years ago) were to live in an expensive house, own an organ, be a published author, hold an executive position, and have a beautiful wife and wonderful children.

God gave me everything! On His scale.

A $50,000 house was modest even back then—but not on my salary! I got an organ, a small Lowry rather than Wurlitzer pipe. I've written about eighteen books—all religious for small markets—no best-selling blockbusters. I was a school principal for twenty-seven years and worked in national ministries—but not an executive in a Fortune 500 company. But by any standards well beyond what I merit, God did give me a beautiful wife and wonderful children.

Am I content? Yes, and I pray that you will be too. And it helps to look not so much at how God has blessed you as it does to see how God has made you a blessing to others. Sort of like what He did for neighbors when I stopped playing the organ.

Just imagine the damage I could have done with a Wurlitzer.

11

Common Unity

Acts 4:32–35

One day, as I was nervously spewing out words and carrying on a conversation with a fellow church worker, I said, "You would think that being in community with one another would result in some common unity! Wait, is that where that word comes from?"

There is community wherever there is common unity! In 2005, the White Sox were in the World Series, and I went with my friend Bob to the United Center to watch game 4 on the big screen. I do not recall how many people were there, but we all were White Sox fans, and I felt pretty comfortable. When the twenty-seventh out was secure in the first baseman's glove, the place exploded with our 1–0 victory! We quickly hopped on the "L" over to the actual stadium, where we celebrated outside with complete strangers. I am usually not comfortable hanging out in a crowd of strangers, let alone talking to and high-fiving them!

It can be hard to find community in a new place or at a new time in life when those around you already have their own communities. Even in a church.

Sometimes churches are more brutally cliquish than the workplace or typical social hangouts. Church members are focused on their own community and forget the overall common unity that has them all gathered in one place. But do not lose hope if you are having trouble finding community. Keep looking!

The reason for our church's Young Adult ministry came from my friend Nathan. Our congregation really had nothing organized for young adults, but it wasn't because we lacked members in that age group. We had many twenty-two- to thirty-year-olds without any kids in the congregation. Some were back home, living with mom and dad. Others were new to the area or in marriage counseling. Then, there was Nathan.

Nathan had been attending worship for a few weeks, sitting by himself in worship and standing awkwardly by himself in the hallway after the service. In the two or three weeks he had visited, no one really talked to him other than the pastor who shook hands with Nathan as he left the sanctuary.

Finally, after those two or three weeks, Andie nudged me and told me to go talk to him. Begrudgingly but dutifully, I went and tried to carry on a conversation. After learning a bit about Nathan's background, I ended up inviting him to go out to the brewery later in the week and talking with him about the possibility of him becoming a youth counselor.

During our conversation, I found out a lot about Nathan. He was a recent college grad working for a big company in town. He had visited all the other churches in town but found something pushing him back toward Zion. Through further conversation, I found out that Nathan was looking for a place to find friends. He had friends at work, but none of them shared the common unity of faith.

Nathan is the reason a large number of young adults began connecting through our Young Adult ministry. His openness and efforts made me realize and understand the need! His persistence, as awkward and embarrassing as it must have been for him, is a testimony to his faith and trust in God. Nathan has become a good friend, and we share community as brothers in faith.

Finding community might be a lesson in persistence. If you haven't found it yet, don't give up. Seek out some common unity. You might have to step outside your comfort zone! Look to the early Christians in Acts 4:32: "Now the full number of those who believed were of one heart and soul, and no one said that any of the things that belonged to him was his own, but they had everything in common."

The Church exists as a gathering place for the community of believers to exist together. Because of our fallen world, even churches fail at times. If you have already found your niche, watch for others who may feel like they are in the margins. The early Christians made sure all the needs were taken care of for everyone in their community.

Who are the Nathans in your life? Maybe you are like Nathan. Pray about your situation, and seek out God's counsel. He has a plan for you. The Father has given us a common unity in the gift of His Son, and we share in the community of believers brought together by the Holy Spirit!

Reflection

Hebrews 10:24–25 is the biblical handbook for creating community: "And let us consider how to stir up one another to love and good works, not neglecting to meet together, as is the habit of some, but encouraging one another, and all the more as you see the Day drawing near."

Implicit in this passage is the fact that it applies to Christian community. Someone in your family probably warned you to be careful about the company you keep, and they were correct. You need Christian community.

None of this is to say that Christians should exclude sinners. You would be back to a group of one—actually zero—if that were the case! Upon examination of Christ's life, you cannot miss His affinity for sinners. The churchy people of the time did not appreciate this reality.

In Him, Christ's followers saw the potential of condemned sinners banding together into a fellowship of forgiven sinners. They were not looking for another god, nor were they looking for like-minded sinners to go out for a roaring good time, all enjoying the same sin together in ways well beyond what they could do alone.

Fellow Christians looking for community may be hard to find. Believers are not always well accepted by the godless unbelievers who outnumber them. Therefore, Aaron's advice is good: look for places where

Christians gather. Church is probably the most obvious.

Like Nathan, you may have to stand around awhile before someone notices. Or, you may have to break some ice yourself and ask to join an existing group. Or, you might have to move to another place where Christians gather. Do not give up.

One more thing: whatever community you find—even if it is a very small community—Jesus promised, "For where two or three are gathered in my name, there am I among them" (Matthew 18:20).

12

No Parking

Hebrews 12:2

Has your car ever been towed? If it has, I'm sure a myriad of possibilities ran through your head when you returned to where your car should be . . . and it was gone!

Initial reactions might include any or all of the following: My car has been stolen! I'm in the wrong parking lot. Or, I'm angry and confused. The sign in front of your chosen parking location or at the front of the lot probably gives you a good explanation, and other than pleading illiteracy, there is little you can do other than call the impound lot where Tommy's Towing has taken your vehicle.

Then anxiety and worry kick in. What time is it? Will the tow company take a credit card? How will I get to the impound lot? Did the towing company really take the car, or was it actually stolen? Why can I park here from 2:00–2:30 p.m. but not from 2:30–2:45 p.m.? Will my car be damaged from the tow?

Tow truck drivers follow the rules almost perfectly. It almost seems as if they are crocodiles waiting for you to park anywhere near those little *No Parking* signs so they can snatch up your vehicle while you are gone. No matter what you say or how you plead, if the tow has begun, there is nothing you can do.

Before we condemn tow truck drivers completely, let's also reflect on how they are also wonderful people. They frequently deal with impatient or frantic people. Whether it involves helping people who locked their keys in their cars, or fixing flat tires, they are usually a blessing to those in need. They might even be moving that pesky person's car who parked in your reserved parking place (whoops!).

It seems like tow truck drivers spend a majority of their time fixing other people's mistakes. They drive in all weather conditions and at all times of day and night. There really isn't a limit to where they are summoned—an urban neighborhood or the middle of a corn field. Tow truck drivers do it all!

At some point in life, you might require some assistance to deal with the despairs and distractions of life. Don't try to fix everything yourself! God gives you many resources to aid your spiritual journey. Most of these resources come in the form of relationships.

Pastors, fellow church members, family, and friends may all be helpful, but keep in mind they are sinners just like you. The only "Tow Truck Driver" able to fix everything is God. And He already has fixed it all.

Hebrews 12:2 tells us, "Looking to Jesus, the founder and perfecter of our faith, who for the joy that was set before Him endured the cross, despising the shame, and is seated at the right hand of the throne of God." Jesus took it upon Himself to fix the problem of sin. He humbled Himself, became a lowly human, and willingly gave His life for you.

Today, find something that reminds you of Jesus every time you look at it. You cannot do this on your own, and sin is a constant distraction. Why not focus on something that reminds you of being fixed too?

I love driving behind the old tow trucks that have what looks like a cross on the back of the truck. It reminds me of Jesus. It reminds me of my failures. It reminds me of His love and the amazing future I have of being "fixed" forever with Him.

Reflection

Not all *No Parking* signs are official. For example, when it snows in Chicago, local residents post their own homemade signs in front of their respective residences. After all, if they take the time and effort to shovel out spaces for their cars in a neighborhood where parking is severely limited, they feel entitled to reserve their spot for themselves. Their *No Parking* signs may be an old chair, a few empty pails, or assorted junk. The penalty for parking is not posted, but there looms a sense of doom for anyone foolish enough to park in their "reserved" spaces.

In one sense, the implied no parking is a lot like guilt. You may not feel the immediate effects of something you have done wrong—or something good you have neglected to do. You may escape dramatic consequences, but guilt tweaks at your memory—and your conscience. Maybe even your anxieties.

Aaron demonstrated how tow trucks are a fitting image for Law and Gospel. They can let you down, or they can lift you up. They represent the hammer of the Law or the rescue of the Gospel.

I was towed once. I honestly did not see the sign, so I was ignorant of my costly infraction. When my car went missing, I desperately searched for a sign. I found it. Too late. Sinners can relate to that experience and feeling. And it did not matter that I met a guy who was searching for his car too—and the sign. I am guessing a lot of people were puzzled over missing cars that day—and the sign they should have seen.

God's Word is your sign. It tells you where not to park your life. And, yes, sometimes you miss the sign. Sometimes you are just having too much fun to see it. Other times, you are blind to it because you are distracted by your needs and wants. Missing or ignoring God's Word always has consequences. Always costly. Sometimes deadly.

God's Word is your sign. Sometimes you see it. Sometimes it is just what you are looking for. Sometimes it just grabs your attention. The Holy Spirit knows when you need it and leads you there. With the psalmist we say, "Oh how I love Your law! It is my meditation all the day" (Psalm 119:97).

God has a vast network of spiritual tow truck drivers. Psalm 91:11 reminds us, “For He will command His angels concerning you to guard you in all your ways.”

Even when your life is parked where is doesn’t belong.

13

Storms of Life

Mark 4:35–41

"But He was in the stern, asleep on the cushion" (Mark 4:38a). How could Jesus have slept inside the boat during a storm?

Back when I was in grade school, my dad received a gift of a fishing excursion on Lake Michigan. He and I always went fishing but never really fished from a boat—and never on Lake Michigan. The day of our excursion, we woke up very early and met up with a group of my friends and their dads. We headed up to the marina where we departed for "a three-hour tour." (I'm not sure how long the trip really was, but the *Gilligan's Island* theme song ran through my head the entire trip.)

Everything started out pretty well. It was a cold day in May, and the water was not calm, but it also wasn't rough by any means. We caught a number of salmon, and we were having a great time. But then a massive storm came up, and, like Gilligan, our tiny ship was tossed! We were still far from shore, and as two- to three-foot waves quickly became six- to ten-foot waves, our dads sent all of us kids inside the boat's cabin. One of my friends was already inside and looking a little green. As soon as I got inside the stuffy cabin, I, too, became a little sick of the sea.

At this point in the story, my memory becomes a little cloudy. Let's just say I was happy they had at least three buckets on board. I vaguely remember looking out the back of the cabin and seeing all the dads holding on as best they could while they used the lake as their "bucket." The storm-fueled waves turned the boat into a seesaw, bouncing forward and back, up and down. Our forty-foot fishing boat continued to be thrown about by the power of the waves. By the time we got back to shore, we were all grateful for land that did not move.

Storms can come up so quickly on a lake. I have been out on the water two or three times when lightning struck nearby. It is very scary! I cannot imagine the horror the disciples felt as the storm tried to claim their fishing boat. Jesus calmed their fears by calming the tempest, but that only created even greater fear in the disciples! Which would you be more frightened by: the storm or the one who with a few words can immediately stop the storm?

Storms create chaos—noise and movement all around. Rain and snow distort your surroundings. Storms bring with them the possibility of danger as well. Trees break, floods sweep away cars and homes, and lightning can cause fires. Storms wreak havoc.

Storms are pretty frequent in the Midwest, as they are in many regions. You cannot do anything to prevent a storm from coming, but you can be prepared.

Life can be stormy as well. These storms come in many different forms and with differing severity. A loved one might die. You might not get the job you worked so hard to get. Financial recessions occur. Violence and terror might happen nearby. Life is full of storms. You cannot prevent them from happening, but you can be prepared.

The aftermath of such storms can send shockwaves through your hopes and dreams. What storms of life are you going through right now? How are they affecting you?

I love the words of Jesus in the Gospel of Mark: "Peace. Be still!" (4:39). The wind stops. The waves stop. The storm just instantly stops! These remarkable words, spoken by our Savior, can be a reassurance for you as you face the storms in your life.

You will always encounter storms in life. Are you prepared? Preparation comes from being still, in Jesus. It comes from focusing on His words and living in His peace. His love and sacrifice create a peaceful calm in the midst of a stormy world. Stay grounded on the Rock; build your foundation upon Him!

Reflection

I hate storms. I worry about the fury of the winds and the drenching of the rain. I worry about hail pockmarking my cars or my siding and lightning setting my house on fire. I worry about loss of power and whether I have enough gas for my generator. I worry a lot.

I worry about my family. We have experienced more than one episode of hunkering in an interior hall. What will happen to us? Where is the dog?

God blessed me with a strong wife who upholds sensibility during the smaller storms that only I fear. (I even fear the forecasts!) And it isn't only the weather. She has seen me through bouts in the emergency room and all the other anxieties of life. Would that God bless every person with a spouse like Renee. Such people are God's gift, especially to those whose weaknesses include timid trust.

The problem with worrying through storms of climate or psyche or spirit is that such behavior suggests a lack of trust in God. "Well, God has helped me through this and that and more, but maybe this time . . . "

Or maybe your thoughts go something like this: "I'm in trouble. God, here is how I want you to get me out of it!" I want Him to handle the storms my way. I miss the rich and full meaning of Romans 8:28: "And we know that for those who love God all things work together for good, for those who are called according to His purpose."

You are called to a purpose. It is not as trite as catching salmon or surviving thunder and lightning or walking out of the ER without assistance. Not that those aren't good things, but they are only part of the big picture of who you are and *Whose* you are.

Sometimes *all things* are not included in your perception of the *best things*. As Shakespeare once wrote, "Therein lies the rub."

The Bible reveals that Paul lived with a "thorn" (2 Corinthians 12:7), certainly something he did not desire. But that thorn was part of the *all things* God used to help Paul through life—a life devoted to proclaiming the Gospel.

So here is a challenge for today: examine your life. Can you identify a few thorns? Take some time to jot down some possibilities.

Was that easy, or did you have a hard time identifying your prickly problems?

The next part of the challenge is more difficult. Can you tell how the thorns—the storms, the frustrations—are serving to help you? Paul said that his thorn was to keep him from becoming conceited. Where are your thorns guiding you?

Aaron's account of the fishing expedition was a thorn to me. For many years, I thought such an adventure would be the epitome of my angling dreams. I realized storms can give you a healthier perspective on epitomes.

As you face both smooth sailing and severe storms, may God bless you with trust and an *all things* perspective. Jesus withstood the worst storm when His Father forsook Him as He fulfilled the work of saving you. He cried in pain, but a few days later He quietly proclaimed the stilling of Satan's storm—the one that almost killed you.

14

Light in the Darkness

1 John 2

"My little children, I am writing these things to you so that you may not sin" (1 John 2:1a).

Those are some big shoes to fill! Good thing John does not stop there. He continues to talk about Jesus being a *propitiation* for our sins.

Propitiation is an interesting word. It implies that something has been done to regain status or favor in the eyes of a higher being. John also uses the word *advocate* in verse two. Both words put the emphasis on Jesus having done everything needed for you not to be sentenced to hell. And yet you still sin. . . . Sin is darkness.

I went camping for the first time the year after I graduated from college. I went with a group of friends to what has to be one of the scariest campsites ever. The campground was about to close for good due to funding cutbacks, so there were random piles of rock in the road, run-down bathrooms, and absolutely no one else camping on our side of the park!

Because we were the sole campers in our area, we arrived at our campsite in complete and utter darkness. Since this was my first time camping, I had no idea what we needed to do to set up a tent or to get a site ready for occupation. I immediately ran to the fire pit and attempted to build a fire to provide some light; however, everything was wet.

I grabbed my little flashlight and held it while my friend Dave attempted to set up the tent, but again my flashlight didn't provide enough light. It was too dark to really accomplish anything!

I decided to unload my car and get the rest of the site set up and ready in case any rain came. I used the key fob to unlock my car—and more than a light bulb came on! Everyone cheered as the headlights pointed directly at the tent, and we easily finished setting it up. How many college grads does it take to set up a tent in the dark? Geesh!

So often, sin not only shrouds our lives but also creates a frenzy in which normal thought processing becomes difficult. To use camping terminology, sin is the darkness that makes it impossible to set up your tent! Light offers a way out.

In 1 John 2:7–11, John explains the battle between light and dark. Light exposes a lot of dirt. It exposes hazards and stumbling blocks. Light pushes the darkness away. Have you ever lit a match in a completely dark room? Immediately, you can begin to make out shapes and outlines. Just a little bit of light can provide insight.

But too often people become trapped in a dark room—the dark room of addiction. Addiction affects everyone in one way or another. At the very least, everyone is addicted to sin. (Did I say least?) In 1 John 2:16–17, John writes:

> For all that is in the world—the desires of the flesh and the desires of the eyes and pride of life—is not from the Father but is from the world. And the world is passing away along with its desires, but whoever does the will of God abides forever.

Desire and addiction are closely related. Adam and Eve were created in God's image, and they were made complete in their relationship with God. But they wanted more.

As sinners, we tend to fill our cravings and desires with worldly things such as sex, drugs, and technology. We turn to what makes us feel good or brings instant relief, rather than focusing on the light of truth Christ provides.

Self-control is a weapon against addiction. Being cognizant of holes or dark spots in your actions and behaviors is a way to work on being self-controlled. Relying on God through trying times is the only way to succeed. Finding an accountability partner can be helpful, but only God can fill those gaps and desires you crave. Adam and Eve were blessed to walk with God—yet they still fell. We have God's Word, His gifts in Baptism and Communion, and the gift of prayer as we live out our "walk" with God.

Addictions may close in like darkness around your life. Trust in God's promises and pray for self-control. "Let what you heard from the beginning abide in you. If what you heard from the beginning abides in you, then you too will abide in the Son and in the Father. And this is the promise that He made to us—eternal life" (1 John 2:24–25).

Reflection

"Got a light?"

Now there is an example when a *light* is not a light! There, the only illumination is at the end of a cigarette—certainly not a light in any biblical sense. Yes, that was my addiction. Took ten years to make it and a year of fierce struggle to break it. It took twenty years for me to get to the point when I no longer had cravings when I drank coffee or was in the presence of someone else who was smoking.

Addiction to smoking is like an addiction to sin. It sneaks up on you. Not that you are totally unaware of what is happening. You just persuade yourself that it is not happening to you. Consequences vary from discomfort and cravings to chronic illness and death.

The light that broke through the darkness of my smoking addiction was my wife. The Light that breaks through my sin habit is the Holy Spirit. Not that I quit sinning, but I have another habit to replace it—repenting!

The path to repentance can be much like Aaron's experience on that dark and desolate campground. Sin facilitates various degrees of panic.

Your early attempts to deal with sin may resemble the stumbling and fumbling Aaron mentioned when first setting up the tent. They attempted the task themselves, without the benefit of light. Fighting sin without the True Light has the same results experienced by the campers. Their repentance came when they stopped trying to fix their own problem and turned to the True Light.

Repentance can be a last resort to finding refuge. Daily repentance blesses us with living in the Light. And if you are like me, you live in lots and lots of Light!

You will continue living in the cycle of sin—repentance—forgiveness in your present phase of life. That is the normal condition of believers as the Holy Spirit guides them through sanctification—the process of becoming holy.

You and I will have one final bout with darkness—the darkness of death. But it will indeed be the *final* bout. It signals the end of your addiction to sin. And that is good news.

Final means the darkness will never confuse, unnerve, or deceive you again. Darkness will disappear. The end is only the end of the old way of life. Then, a new life begins.

Just listen, "And night will be no more. They will need no light of lamp or sun, for the Lord God will be their light, and they will reign forever and ever" (Revelation 22:5).

15

What's Your Number?

Romans 13:7–10

What is your number? No, not your phone number or address. What is your debt number?

Sadly, you might spend your first ten or fifteen years after graduation paying off student loans, credit card debt, or car loans.

In 2014, the average student loan debt was $33,000 (www.debt.org/students). Add that amount to other possible debts, and the average college grad could be $50,000 in debt! So much for putting a down payment on a house, starting a savings account, or tithing! Any extra funds are probably going straight to debt payment.

People find it almost impossible to live without carrying debt. Mortgages, credit cards (even paying off the balance!), and personal loans are all forms of debt. Debt can feel like a giant weight on your shoulders, never letting up. Debt seems to create a hopeless spiral down into the financial abyss.

In his letter to the Romans, Paul talks about debt:

> Pay to all what is owed to them: taxes to whom taxes are owed, revenue to whom revenue is owed, respect to whom respect is owed, honor to whom honor is owed. Owe

> no one anything, except to love each other, for the one who loves another has fulfilled the law. (Romans 13:7–8)

Paul encouraged believers to not have any debt. But in today's culture, debt seems almost an inevitable reality for the twenty-something. You need a college degree to land a well-paying job. You need reliable transportation to get to that job. Rent feels like a waste of money when you could be paying the same amount for a mortgage and actually gaining some equity.

Racking up debt is never a good idea, even if it seems a necessity. It's even more important to make your payments in full and in a timely manner. There is hope!

I was blessed to start life after college with no debt in my name. My college education was paid through scholarships and by my parents. Their sacrifices and healthy financial decisions—especially on two church-worker salaries—allowed me to keep the cost of my education from being a burden after I graduated. I am eternally grateful to them!

I had a tiny but reliable Dodge Neon to drive around, and I lived in a modest apartment the first five years after graduation. I really did not encounter debt until a few years later when I decided to buy a new car to replace the once reliable, now unreliable Neon. This was a major financial move and might have been the cause for me taking a trip to the ER that night (or, more likely, it was the burger I had at lunch that day . . .). Either way, signing up for $20,000 of debt was a little unnerving. As my six-year payment plan continued, those car payments were built in to my budget and were never really a burden.

The next debt I amassed was our wedding. Our wedding was beautiful, awesome, and I would never change a thing—but it did cost money. Again, my parents paid a large portion of the total amount, but Andie and I still accrued an intimidating balance on our credit cards.

Our debt got quickly out of hand. While we managed to pay off what we spent each month, our old debt was not really diminishing. Major changes were in order: we canceled cable, only went out to eat once a month, and watched our spending at the grocery store. At the same time, we were dealing with the house we didn't live in (remember chapter 3?), Andie's student loans, and new jobs. It felt like our debt had become like one of those sponge toys that starts off in a tiny capsule and continues to grow and expand while soaking overnight. We were not spending frivolously; there simply wasn't enough money coming in!

We put a plan in place. We started a monthly spending budget, which included *debt* as one of the line items. This became a great framework to paying off the ridiculous interest rates of credit cards. With those paid off, the rest of our loans seemed so much more manageable. We are still not completely debt free, but money is no longer controlling our every decision.

Paul knew the power that debt can hold over you. That is why he focused on being in debt in a different way. A modern paraphrase of his words in Romans might say, "Love one another—do not just focus on yourself! Loving one another is a fulfillment of the law—love God and love one another."

If paying off fiscal debt is a priority, loving one another should be viewed in the same way. Being in debt to love one another puts a different urgency on the command. Do not put off being an example of love to your neighbor. Be urgent and intentional in your actions today. Who is someone you can love? How does knowing the love of Christ help you fulfill this directive?

Christ paid our debt to sin in full. He paid with His blood and with His life. He did this willingly. He did so with you in mind. It was not a simple exchange of payment for debt. It was a difficult road, a struggle up the hill of Golgotha, and a sacrifice. He did all that because He loves you and wants you to live free from the debt that Satan wants to hold over your head. He took the weight of your sin on His shoulders and heaved it off when He defeated death. Don't let debt be your prison; let the debt Christ paid be your motivation to share His love with others!

Reflection

You cannot always rely on someone's generosity or resources. Sometimes there is little of either.

Sometimes I regret the financing I provided for my children. Just think of the car I could be driving, the house I could have on a lake, the vacations, the . . . Thanks be to God, the regrets do not last long.

I am not wealthy. Yet God has given Renee and me a godly perspective on money. And He has given us hearts for family and the generosity that, in our minds, goes with it. Love prevails even amid scarcity of resources.

Generosity. I hope you have it. Generosity is a wonderful, uplifting experience. But a lot can get in its way, fun and fear being two culprits. Fun may boil down to expensive pursuits of pleasure, which when practiced in ungodly ways can lead to all sorts of problems—including an expansion of that debt number.

Fear? If I am generous, will I have enough for myself? A healthy concern? Yes. Fear? No. For some biblical insight, see the story of the Widow of Zarephath in 1 Kings 17:8–16 or consider the generosity of the widow whose church offering was about a penny—all that she had, given with no inkling of how she would make it through the next day (Luke 21:1–3).

Do not allow numbers to cripple your service to others. Your numbers will get better. After all, someday you will come into a big inheritance—not because of your generosity but because of your Father's.

"And now I commend you to God and to the word of His grace, which is able to build you up and to give you the inheritance among all those who are sanctified" (Acts 20:32).

16

Rest and Retreat

Mark 2:23–27

You might want to read this chapter at bed time.

"And on the seventh day God finished His work that He had done, and He rested on the seventh day from all His work that He had done" (Genesis 2:2).

Even God rested.

God took a full six days, from morning to evening, to create the spectacular world we live in. He also took a full day, morning to evening, to rest after that astonishing week. Now if God took a full day to rest, what about you?

If you are just starting out in a job, your days of rest are probably few and far between. Starting a new job generally requires an extra effort on your part to gain experience, influence, and establish some credibility in your work environment. A day off is not high on the priority list. But even if you work weekends, your employer should allow for one or two days off each week. Be sure to take that time seriously and intentionally. Avoid the temptation to overschedule your time off.

I try to guard my days off, or at least create a schedule that allows me a different day of rest if I have obligations on my normal day off. I find if I do not have a dedicated time to recover and relax, I start to lag behind or develop a negative attitude. I need a full day off—even an hour-long work obligation can derail my efforts the next week.

Have you ever taken a vacation with such a jam-packed schedule that you returned more tired than when you left? It's not an uncommon experience. If you go to a new place, you want to see everything that place has to offer. If you return to a place you've been before, you want to do some of the things you did last time along with more that you were unable to do the previous trip. Do you build time for rest into your vacations?

If you think you are busy now, just wait. What do you do in your free time? Countless times I have been with people of different ages and situations who have similar answers to this question. Whether retired, still working to support a family, married, or single, the answers are always the same. For parents and grandparents, free time is often filled with running kids from one end of town to the other for music lessons or sporting events. For others, free time is spent caring for aging parents, going to friends' weddings, or sitting all day at volleyball tournaments. People are too busy! Most people enjoy their activities, and it is good to be active and out doing things, but time quickly becomes a fragile commodity.

God did not create us to constantly be in a flurry of activity. He created us with a need for rest! He even commands us to rest in the Third Commandment.

In Mark 2, the Pharisees are having a discussion with Jesus. Actually, it was more like an attempted entrapment. After all, the disciples were doing "work" on the Sabbath! Jesus' response is one we all need to remember. He said, "The Sabbath was made for man, not man for the Sabbath" (Mark 2:27). God knew His uniquely created people would need rest. He knows how easily we get burned out. God promises us, "Come to Me, all who labor and are heavy laden, and I will give you rest" (Matthew 11:28).

You need rest. To help make resting easier, consider these strategies:

Take a sharpie and block out your days off. It will be much easier to say no to new appointments when you can't write them on your calendar.

Develop a routine for your days off. Find a coffee shop or park where you can do an activity that recharges you.

Find a hobby. No one has time for hobbies anymore; it is a disappearing art.

Spend time in God's Word and in prayer.

If you have to do chores around the house, be sure to make time to relax.

Develop a habit of physical exercise.

Find an accountability partner to keep you focused on rest.

Jesus took time to rest also. After His work on the cross was finished, He rested in the tomb. His job was complete. He did not stay in that tomb though. He burst forth and continued His mission to love people and be God's grace to a hurting world. Rest assured in His sacrifice and His love.

Reflection

As I remember, Aaron was not one for resting as a baby or young child. He was a nap rebel, always having a hard time falling sleep. He had no idea that he would be writing this devotion someday. If he had, he probably would have gotten more sleep!

You live a dual life. You relish rest and yet you undervalue it. You know you need it—just not how much. And note—rest is more than sleeping in on Saturday mornings or finding the reverend's voice so soothing during a Sunday service that you . . .

As you age—yes, you are aging right now—your need for rest becomes more apparent and more vital. You are not invulnerable.

Rest, however, can be overrated and even abused. Consider the wise words of Proverbs 6:9–11:

> How long will you lie there, O sluggard?
> When will you arise from your sleep?
> A little sleep, a little slumber,
> a little folding of the hands to rest,
> and poverty will come upon you like a robber,
> and want like an armed man.

Another abuse of rest evolves when you find yourself resting from spiritual needs and practices. Too tired to pray at bedtime? Too foggy to pray when you get up? Sleeping in and neglecting worship? Too tired of your own problems to help a friend with his?

Praise God that He does not tire of forgiving you and sending His Spirit to empower you. He gives you work, *and* He gives you rest!

Praise God that He is God and that He has not rested since that very first seventh day on the calendar. If you want an idea of what He has on His daily activity list, take a look at Isaiah 40:28–31.

God is God, and you are not. Trust fully in Him to get His work done. He has lots of experience. Do your work and enjoy your entertainment, but make rest a significant *other* in the schedule to which you are married!

Oh, and that prayer thing I mentioned before? Martin Luther, a man of many hours also knew how to rest. In the Daily Prayer section of his Small Catechism, after making suggestions on how to end the day and providing a marvelously comprehensive prayer in less than seventy-five words, Luther concludes with this: "Then go to sleep at once and in good cheer." (Small Catechism, Evening Prayer).

A very, very good night to you!

17

Who's Looking Back at You?

Isaiah 45:9

When you last looked in the mirror did you recognize the person staring back at you?

Society has a self-image problem. There is pressure to wear tighter, more fashionable clothing. It's even acceptable to show your underwear! I remember when "sagging" was popular. Do you know how hard it is to walk with your pants hanging that low? Stock in belts must have taken a nosedive with that terrible fad!

Society must like illusions. I am not a specialist, but one only needs to stumble upon the infomercials to discover there are shapewear and slimming garments to help conceal the natural you. Thanks to modern technology, many celebrity photos are touched up to remove all blemishes—including features that may not be blemishes!

When Andie and I arrived in Michigan, we had to get our picture taken for the church directory. I am not a fan of pictures. I usually end up making memorably goofy faces rather than just behaving myself and smiling. I also rarely say, "That's a bad picture of me." When we had our photograph taken, the photographer offered a ten-dollar add-on/touch-up. My instinct was to say "No!" but we were in a basement, and the lighting did not appear to be so good, so we agreed and forked up the extra cash.

Now, I know my manners well enough to never tell a woman she has taken a bad picture, but when we received the pictures and saw them in the directory, I was with a different person. Andie did not look like herself. Rather, she looked *so* different due to the professional "touch-up" that I thought the photographer sent us the wrong photograph!

Who was this extremely fake-looking person in the photo? Andie is beautiful and has dimples and freckles. I have messed around with photo editing software enough to know it can be fun, but you can also absolutely change the reality of the image. The person in the photo appeared to have no neck, was very flat-faced, and had a bizarre, awkward-looking smile.

Isaiah 45:9 says, "Woe to him who strives with Him who formed him, a pot among earthen pots! Does the clay say to him who forms it, 'What are you making?' or 'Your work has no handles'?" Why argue with the Creator? That photo of Andie did not need touching up. And while the touch-up changed what she looks like, it did not change who she is—a loved child of God.

Media and society might tell you to guard against self-image problems, but do not let your appearance affect your self-worth. Jesus died for all. In fact, "While we were still sinners, Christ died for us" (Romans 5:8b). Sin has destroyed the perfect bodies that God created in Adam and Eve. Sin attempts to destroy your value as a loved and redeemed child of God too.

You have value. Do not let anyone tell you differently. You are a cherished prize of the Creator, worth the blood of His Son. So next time you look in a mirror, I hope you see a person loved by Jesus.

Reflection

Renee and I have lived in the house where we raised Aaron and Allison for more than thirty years. That means we have looked in the same mirror for more than thirty years. My observation is that the mirror got old, not me. What else could you expect after three decades?

An old expression suggests that "mirrors don't lie." You cannot dispute this truth, but equally true is the fact that mirrors don't tell all. For example, there is a lot more to me than a thinning head of hair and thickening hair in the nose and on the ears.

Do not mock! You will be there some day!

Mirrors do not tell all. Oh, the expression on your face or the way you comb your hair or how you apply your make-up or shave your beard may reveal something of the inner you. But so much more lies beyond the surface.

What do friends and family see that your mirror cannot? Do people around you see mostly smiles or frowns? Mostly contentment or anxiety? Mostly smugness or humility? Mostly saint or sinner?

Imagine God is on the backside of that mirror. What does He see? Whoopee? Or uh-oh? Good, kind, and considerate? Or bad, mean, and rude?

God sees it all. How do you feel about that?

God knows all your bad. Were He a computer user, He would need to add gigabyte after gigabyte of storage space to contain the size of spreadsheet needed to keep track of your sins. Sometimes we are confronted with so much data it seems impossible to comprehend the enormity of our condition.

Not so with God. He gets it all. He has seen past the mirror from the day you were born until now, as you are reading this and perhaps thinking a few negatives thoughts about the writer who calculates your sins without even knowing you!

What would you see if you looked in the mirror right now? If not anger, then fear? Apathy?

Those would be normal reactions when confronted by sin. Then, of course, there are the unbelievers or the delusional who do not see a sinner in the mirror. They really do not think they have a self-image problem. They are to be pitied and prayed for.

So why all this talk about the seamy you? (Bet you have never been called that to your face!) There is, however, a wonderful reason for it. Despite the ugliness of your sin, God loves you. His love did not begin with the perfect you at birth, for you had already inherited sinfulness (Romans 5:12)—even though your aunt thought you were the cutest thing in the world. His love for you did not begin when you "straightened out" by coming back to church or reading religious books. His love for you began long before you were born (Jeremiah 1:5).

So what does God see when He looks at you?

He sees a Christian. Unlike some worldly definition of Christians, He does not see a perfectly moral and upstanding human being. He sees a forgiven sinner instead. He sees one of His children, not just touched up, but truly transformed by the blood of Jesus, whose sacrifice paid for your sins and nudged you down the road to a perfection that you will fully realize in your next phase of life.

Go ahead. Glare down what Satan wants you to see in the mirror. See instead yourself—with Jesus standing next to you. You will not find a greater way to start your day.

18

Betrayal

1 Corinthians 11:23–26

Betrayal has to be the worst feeling in the world.

Betrayal hurts most from those you care about. It is almost a form of torture. The lingering emotional effects can last for days, months, or even years. When you trust someone, you give him or her an open door to your heart and life. When that trust is betrayed, it might feel like a piece of you has died. Betrayal is a relationship killer.

Jesus knew all too much about betrayal. Scripture tells us how Judas and Peter, along with the rest of the disciples, seemed to desert Jesus in His time of trial. If the emotions associated with betrayal were not enough pain, Jesus was physically tortured as well.

Betrayal cannot be avoided. It will happen at some point in your life, and you cannot do anything to stop it. Of course, you can be sure not to betray anyone yourself, but when it comes to others, you simply cannot control their actions. As a response to betrayal, it can be easy to wallow in your depression and dwell on the loss. Sometimes it's easy to put up walls to prevent betrayal from ever happening again.

During my freshman year of high school, I really liked this one particular girl. Within a week of school starting, I told a friend of mine who unfortunately thought it was a joke and quickly proceeded to tell the whole school. After that incident, I used more discretion with whom I trusted.

In ministry, I have had relationships with families that I thought existed beyond the church walls. Instead these families have shown me that our relationships are more professional than personal. I lived life with those people, shared my weaknesses, drove their kids around, and made personal sacrifices, all to have it thrown back in my face.

I have had pastors throw me to the wolves before hearing me out. Shouldn't the Church look different? Even in the family of Christ, must we have to choose whom we can trust? Unfortunately, betrayal is all too frequent in life and even in ministry.

Now that I have been real with you, let us look at Jesus' experience with betrayal. "On the night when He was betrayed . . ." (1 Corinthians 11:23).

These words often get lost in the repetition. On that same night when Jesus was betrayed, He had fellowship with those who were going to betray Him. Jesus knew exactly who was going to betray Him and how it would happen! If you knew you were about to be betrayed, would you have dinner with that person? I certainly would not. I would run away or expose the betrayal before it happened. Not Jesus. He simply reclined, had dinner with His disciples, and gave them a foretaste of the feast to come. He gave them forgiveness and served them in His humility!

I encourage you to do everything possible to build healthy relationships founded on trust and love. When betrayal happens, remember that Jesus died for His betrayers, your betrayers, and especially you. He gave His body and blood to those who turned their backs on Him. He loved them. He forgave them.

You have betrayed Christ too. The devil works hard to present you opportunities to sin against God and His commands. Yet Jesus offers you the same love and forgiveness He offered His disciples. Every time you hear the words "given and shed for you," remember His forgiveness and love.

Christ has been betrayed. You have been betrayed. Remember the gifts Christ gives you as He strengthens you through the Holy Spirit found in God's Word and Sacraments. There we see and experience the forgiveness given us through faith in Christ.

Reflection

Unless you are inclined toward evil, you do not intend to betray anybody. But it happens.

Infamous betrayers include names like Marcus Brutus, Benedict Arnold, Marshal Pétain, and most famous of all: Judas Iscariot.

Brutus killed his BFF, Julius Caesar, in a misguided and treacherous attempt to keep him from becoming the kind of ruler that he opposed. Arnold turned against his troops—the American troops he once led—because of hurt feelings. Pétain sold out France to Hitler. Everybody knows Judas's story. You might understand how someone could betray his country, but how could anyone betray Jesus? Of course Judas could not understand Jesus' true purpose, and that caused the problem.

Often, betrayal is not blatant. Rather, more descriptive terms might be *insidious* or even *incidental*. Consider those occasions when you are most prone to betraying a best friend, a family member, the public trust, or even Jesus!

Family member? Best friend? They are among the easiest to betray because each trusts you from their hearts, and it's trust built over the passage of much time. What do such betrayals look like?

Failure to keep appointments might be one. Have you promised a child that you would be there for her dance recital or his basketball game? Have children or friends not called you when they knew you were down in the dumps or when they failed to show up for your party? Relational apathy or taking friendships for granted is perhaps chief among betrayals.

Public trust? Has a licensing agency deemed you capable of driving? Their assumption is that you will obey traffic laws. Okay, so we will not even go there, but sometimes even "minor" betrayals can have severe consequences.

Jesus? Et tu? When you consider that Jesus loved you so much that He lived, sacrificed, and even died for you, the connection between betrayal and sin is clear. Your sins were among those that nailed Him to the cross. Jesus was abandoned not only by His Father but also by believers who knew and know He loves them but still sinned anyway.

And then there is apathy. Is it not easy to take Jesus for granted? After all, His forgiveness is legendary. Maybe you forget to talk to Him for a few weeks, which can grow to a few months, which can grow to . . .

Feel bad about such things. But do not despair.

Feeling bad leads to repentance—the only reliable way to address betrayal. Sorrow and re-commitment happens a lot with sinners because of our inability to perfect our lives. Yet, God loves sinners so much that He never runs out of forgiveness. Even for sins of betrayal.

Jesus will never betray you. No, that sentence is not to prompt an ending like, "So think twice about betraying Him." You can think about your sins as many times as you wish, and it will not cure you. In fact, it will convict you. Jesus will never betray you. What a comfort! Just think, when the proverbial meeting between you and God takes place at the pearly gates and God asks why He should let you in, Jesus will say, "He is with me."

19

Lambs, Wolves, and Lions

1 Peter 5:8–9

The Book of 1 Peter abounds with animals. Peter mentions lambs, wolves, serpents, and scorpions.

When Jesus sent out the seventy-two disciples, He compared them to lambs among wolves. Anyone knowing anything about the food chain understands that lambs will not last long against a pack of hungry wolves. The wolves will hunt the lambs, surround them, and then feed on them. A lamb is defenseless unless a shepherd is nearby. Jesus gave His disciples a warning, knowing that they would be rejected, hated, and even persecuted in their efforts to spread the kingdom of God. (But look at the heading before Luke 10:17 . . . all seventy-two return!)

Do you think of yourself as prey? Was your blessing from your pastor at confirmation time, "Go, be a lamb among wolves"?

The world can be a scary place. The devil makes sure that danger abounds. His legions of demons and other fallen creatures often wreak havoc upon God's creation. The devil himself "prowls around like a roaring lion, seeking someone to devour" (1 Peter 5:8). I would much rather take my chances against a wolf!

All too often though, the world wants to put Satan on the same level as God. God knows our hearts, our intentions, and He knows our thoughts.

Satan does not. He is just a created being. God has always been and will always be. Satan is a fallen angel. In fact, in Luke 10:18, Jesus tells the seventy-two, "I saw Satan fall like lightning from heaven." He continues by talking about the power and authority he gave the seventy-two over the forces of evil.

You have that same power. As a redeemed child of God, you belong to Him. The devil can tempt you and make sin look awfully appealing, but he cannot force you to give in!

Satan does not know your thoughts and cannot read your mind, but he does know where you have failed in the past and attempts to exploit your weaknesses. His weapon is lies. He offers false promises and obscure justifications, and he loves to think he has power over you. John even calls him the "father of lies" (John 8:44). But as Martin Luther reminds us, "One little word can fell him" (*LSB* 656:3).

Think of one word that will remind you that you belong to God and say it often . . . *liar* . . . *NO* . . . *redeemed* . . . *Jesus* . . . whatever one word reminds you that you belong to God.

When temptations come around, be confident that the devil does not have power over you. Resist him with the strength given you by the Holy Spirit. Don't let the devil get a foothold. Rather, build your foundation on the Good Shepherd.

Reflection

Think about the word *animals*. What images or emotions does that word bring to mind? *Animals* is a great Law/Gospel word. This one word powers emotions and images from fierce and fearsome to affectionate and cuddly. You can also use *animals* to describe the students in an unsupervised middle school lunchroom or a crate of puppies.

Our family always has been fond of animals—exclusive, naturally, of animals that will not return the mutual feelings.

When I was a child, I spent a few days on a farm owned by the family of my sister's fiancé. Being a city boy, every farm animal harbored potential for vicious violence—even chickens. Yes, chickens. I was asked to feed the chickens and given a bucket of feed to do so. With not a chicken in sight, I opened the gate to their enclosure. I think it was an ambush, as a few of the beasts rushed me. I flung the feed at them and banged on the bucket, which brought *all* the chickens out in a mad rush. The devils! To this day, I keep my distance from the frozen chicken case at the market.

As you can tell, I escaped to tell the story today. I survived to share what it is like to be pursued by "cackling chickens seeking someone to devour." (This also explains why you will not find the book of 1 Edward in the Bible.)

I am happy that Aaron never had to face a horde of fowl. But he—and you—and I do face the foulest of enemies. Peter's passage about a "roaring lion" is not just some old piece of metaphorical musing. It remains as true today as it was in Peter's time.

The bad thing about the lions that pursue us is that often they do not look like lions. Would that Satan's minions look fierce and frightening. Would that all sins be bloody, slimy, and putrid. But Satan and sin do not work that way. They live lives that appear affectionate and cuddly. They lick but never bite. At least not until they can deliver suffering or even death.

You will face many roaring lions in disguise. You live in a zoo filled with a menagerie that tempts you to think of them as household pets. But they are behind bars for a reason.

Picture God's Word—and God's words—as the fence that stands between you and the roaring lions. The more you know about that fence, the more confident you can be as you face life's woes equipped with your own set of "Whoas!" as sin attempts to draw you in.

You also will face roaring lions that pretend no disguise. They are the in-your-face enemies of God's Word—and words. You probably have met a few already. They may be those from whom you learned—the ones with many letters behind their names as credentials of their wisdom and authority. They are the ones who mocked God as a fantasy and a psychological crutch for believers like you. Did you challenge them? You know about roaring lions!

Did you not challenge them? Does it bother your conscience, or are you happy to have escaped with a good grade? Did you decide that roaring lions could not hear you even if you presented stunning testimony of your faith? Discretion may indeed be the better part of spiritual valor, as long as the roaring lions did not recruit you to be part of their pride.

Friends may pose a threat too. They have the ability to both roar and purr. No, do not run off and cloister yourself. The Bible reminds us that we need to be in the world but not of the world (Mark 16:15; Romans 12:2). Be an animal but don't be an *animal*!

The faith God has given to you is meant to be shared. It is intended to "feed the animals," so to speak. They may rush you like a bunch of angry chickens. But who knows?

Maybe they are just hungry!

20

First Impressions

Colossians 4:5–6

One of my favorite activities to do with Andie is people watch. People sure are interesting! We have accumulated quite a few stories from our people-watching excursions—such as the time a fight broke out and was quickly snuffed out by a few army reservists dining near us. Another time, a waiter carrying a tray of food had a seizure and was almost trampled by a customer who reacted very poorly. Then there was the couple on a first date. They were sitting next to us in the restaurant, and there was absolutely no conversation taking place—it was incredibly awkward! Sometimes, when Andie and I are not entirely sure what's transpiring, we like to make up our own backstory. (Be careful if you ever come across us in a restaurant!)

I often spend my mornings at our local coffee shop. A lot of interesting people like to stop in and grab coffee. I have seen politicians, artists, professors, and people sporting a variety of different lifestyles. No matter who the person is or what he or she looks like, there is one scenario that never goes smoothly: meeting a blind date for the first time!

It never gets old watching people walk in and scope out the joint like they know who they are looking for before they accept the fact that they have no idea what their target looks like!

Oftentimes, I am asked if I am Tony or Alex, and well . . . no. (One time I almost said yes just to see what the date was about!) I, too, have been in that situation a few times myself, not having a clue for whom I was looking. Short of Facebook stalking, it is nearly impossible to know what someone will look like from just hearing his or her voice or reading an email. Even profile pictures prove to not be very helpful because the person might look very different in real life.

Chances are you will have some of these same encounters. Entering a different world and starting a new life means you will be making a host of first impressions.

How does God want you to come across? Colossians 4:5–6 says, "Walk in wisdom toward outsiders, making the best use of the time. Let your speech always be gracious, seasoned with salt, so that you may know how you ought to answer each person." That message definitely goes beyond first impressions and should be a standard for how the family of believers treats not only one another but everyone!

Is your conversation tasteful? Does your first—or eighty-third—impression leave positive memories with the other person? Do you look different from the world in a "salty" way? Christ's followers should appear different.

On an episode of the television show *Chopped!* there was a chef who made it clear that his life was changed because of Jesus. When he won, he gave away his $10,000 prize to the other contestant, who was heartbroken that she would not get to travel to see a family member without winning. The judges were shocked. Their mouths hung open, not understanding this act of kindness. Did that contestant convert everyone in the room or everyone watching the show? Probably not, but he did leave a lasting impression of who he was—and shared a powerful message of what it means to be a Christ-follower.

As you go about meeting people for the first time, be mindful of your impressions. Be so salty that you witness through your conversation and through your actions. God lives in you! May the Holy Spirit empower you to love, to serve, and to boldly proclaim the love of Christ in all you do. Remember, you never know who is watching!

Reflection

My first impression of Aaron was that he was tiny and noisy. Of course, you could say the same of nearly all newborns. His squawking gave his doctor the impression that he would be a lawyer. I disagreed. My impression was that he would become a preacher. Renee's impression was that he would be neither; he would just be Aaron. A team of doctors assembled in the delivery room to give their impressions about the health of this premature child. Their impressions were good.

Not so good is the impression we all give upon birth.

Okay, there is Aunt Olga, who sees you as a wonderful specimen of humankind, perfect in every way—though she has never changed a diaper. She is in good company because many people believe that children are born perfect—and that they can only get better. That belief reflects the teaching and philosophy of secular humanism—or kind but tainted religious teaching—rather than the stark reality painted by accurate biblical worldview. But back to the reality of first impressions.

God's first impression of you is that you are a miserable, unclean sinner. Ouch. Except, apparently, for some dinner clients, that is not the first impression you want to leave on others. The truth hurts, and Scripture proclaims it (Genesis 8:21; Psalm 51:5): You were born in sin. And even if you were not born that way, it would not have taken you long to earn your own (Matthew 15:19). This is God's first impression of you: "And you were dead in the trespasses and sins" (Ephesians 2:1).

You can take no comfort in knowing that God's first impression of you is the same of His first impression of everybody. But just as your parents loved you despite your newborn wrinkles and rankles, God loved you so much that "while we were still weak, at the right time Christ died for the ungodly. . . . But God shows His love for us in that while we were still sinners, Christ died for us" (Romans 5:6, 8).

The first impression you left upon God has been replaced by a new and improved you! You see, your ability to leave a new perfect impression is not something you acquired through your own good personality or by reading books on how to win friends and influence people. The new you is a result of a makeover—a makeover earned by Jesus through His perfect life, sacrificial death, and victorious resurrection.

The new you should impress others from the first time they meet you and throughout your relationships with them. But *should* is a hard word.

In one sense—the sense that is personal to you—your ongoing sinful nature prevents you from making good, lasting impressions, even if you make great first impressions. You are not completely perfect. Yet.

In another sense, you may find others not liking their first impressions of you, even if to others they are righteous first impressions. This may happen when you really want to leave a great first impression for whatever reason. You already know that some people do not want to keep company with Christians like you. It happened to Jesus too!

None of this needs to prevent you from leaving godly first and lasting impressions on others. Just shake out more salt.

21

Waiting for Contentment

Philippians 4:11–13

When I was young, I prayed for patience. When I was older, I prayed that I would have to stop waiting for things to happen! As I grew older, I learned firsthand that if you wait for contentment it will never come. In searching for that time of peace and satisfaction, I definitely learned patience, but it certainly was a struggle.

When my situation in central Illinois was deteriorating rapidly, I found myself spending more time at Panera than in the church office. Even now I tend to do a lot of work offsite, but back then I was going places to avoid the office completely, not to interact with people in the community. I was unquestionably *not* content and *not* happy with my circumstances.

My name had been on a call list for a few years already. I had interviewed at what seemed to be probably forty times. I made the short list at many places and had even visited a few, but had not received any offers. A reality was sinking in that I might have to stay in central Illinois, drop out of the ministry, and do something different with my life.

But God had different plans!

Finally, I received job offer to a central Indiana location. This was not very exciting. If there is anything more boring than the landscape in central Illinois, it's the landscape in central Indiana! Regardless of the surroundings, I had finally received a call! In college they teach you never to run away from your current call—but my feet were already moving; my decision had been made!

That is . . . until I received the paperwork. Again, they teach you in college not to base decisions on reasons such as finances and location but rather on the job description and the Holy Spirit's influence. However, the salary and insurance package equaled about a $10,000 reduction in pay. Andie and I had been married just a few months, and we had plenty of debt hanging over our heads. A major cut in my salary and a few months with no income from Andie would have been deadly for us.

I struggled. Everything about this job offer was a life-saver: the timing, the position itself, the proximity to our families, and the possibility of actually doing ministry again all made me want to say *yes*! But the uncertainties weighed heavily on my mind. *Where would Andie get a job? How could we cut back on spending? Could we actually make ends meet on such a small amount of money? What if the dynamics of this call ended up being the same as the one I was already in?*

I was torn. My mind raced. I could not sleep. I could not work. The joy and excitement of potential escape was tremendous, but reality was overwhelming.

I remember everything about the moment I discovered the definition of contentment. I was at a car dealership waiting on an oil change and reading a book about contentment. I had made a pros and cons list, done SWOT analysis, and prayed unceasingly. The problem was I wanted so badly to leave that I did not even consider the alternative of staying. Sitting at a table with three other people, I broke down in tears. They were tears of sorrow but also of relief. What if I stayed? The decision was clear. This was not the right time for my exodus. I would stay.

A sense of peace flowed through me.

A sorrowful calm enveloped me.

I would be content in my current situation.

Contentment is a decision. It is a choice to be satisfied and at peace regardless of the circumstances. In his letter to the Philippians, Paul writes that he has endured many different situations and has learned the secret of being content, "I can do all things through Him who strengthens me" (Philippians 4:13).

It is not easy to be content. It requires a conscious effort to go beyond your own desires, to dialogue with God, and to finally accept the challenges of life. Trusting God goes a long way in being content.

When I finally gave the decision to God, I knew He would give me the power to continue. He would rescue me in His time. A few months later, I received the call to Michigan. During the wait, I found Psalm 37 helpful in directing my trust to God. God is faithful. He loves you and cares for you. Let Him strengthen you to make a decision of contentment.

Reflection

So many factors influence job-related decisions. Church workers, like Aaron and the rest of our family, seem to have additional considerations due to what is known as a *call*—a system of connecting professional church workers with congregations. Entering the mix of decision-making considerations are scriptural and spiritual factors, as well as organizational policies and practices.

I do not believe that jobs and vocations outside of professional church work are exempt from scriptural and spiritual factors.

Paul did not write to professional church workers alone; he wrote to all the Christians living in Philippi, and he wrote for Christians in all places and careers for all times. The concept is called vocation, and it involves what God has called you to do, whether it is stockbroker, trucker, dog walker, CIO, mechanic, and so on.

God created you for service (Ephesians 2:10). Whatever good things you do through your work qualify as godly service. Wow. That sentence has serious implications.

First, consider the career and job options available to you. If you are blessed with choices, pray for wisdom in choosing wisely, and consider what God can do through the skills and knowledge with which He has blessed you.

Second, your work must be the highest quality you have to offer. In other words, you must be "all in." Not surprisingly, an "all in" work ethic usually leaves a favorable impression and a positive portfolio with management. When you work in the name of Jesus, you do good works that bring glory to God and bless those you serve.

Third, those who work around you and who are served by you know who you are and *Whose* you are. This is no guarantee they will like you or help you climb the ladder to success. But they will know that you are a disciple of Christ.

Oh . . . about contentment. As Aaron intimated, it can be hard to obtain. You need to trust this: "I can do all things through Him who strengthens me" (Philippians 4:13)—one of the most misunderstood Bible passages. This is neither a promise that you will achieve total success nor some kind of resigned "it is what it is" contentment. It is a promise that God will strengthen you to deal with all things life throws at you.

God bless you in all that He calls you to do.

22

Curfew

Proverbs 1:7–9

Proverbs 1:8–9 says, "Hear, my son, your father's instruction, and forsake not your mother's teaching, for they are a graceful garland for your head and pendants for your neck."

Now, I've never liked wearing necklaces, but I imagine this proverb as a link to the Fourth Commandment's promise of long life. Obedience is a major emphasis of childhood. You must obey your parents, you have to follow the rules of the road, you have to be this tall in order to ride that ride, and so forth. Rules abound while you are shaping and molding your identity. The guidelines set by your family largely influenced who you have become.

I had four and arguably even five parents growing up. Other than my mom and dad, my grandma also lived with us. My sister was also a parent to me for as long as I can remember. Even Millie the dog barked orders at me—literally! Despite all the structure and order that a household of four adults and one mothering dog offered, I rebelled. I often hid away in my room or stayed out late with friends.

One of the first times I was allowed to stay out late, I returned home four minutes past my curfew. What I thought was a minuscule infraction was actually a violation of family law that resulted in the maximum penalty:

a four-week grounding, one week for each minute I was late. Let me tell you, I never came home past my curfew again!

That certainly was not the last time I disobeyed my parents though. I thought I knew better and could create a better life for myself based on my own rules. Looking back, I realize why order and structure were in place. My parents—all of them except the dog—were trying to give me the best start they could, as well as foster an environment in which I could succeed in life.

God does the same for you, but the rules He set in place are not simply guidelines for life. One simple violation deserves the maximum penalty. In order to obtain eternal life, one has to be perfect, and only One actually was perfect—Jesus. His perfect obedience as the Son of God and Son of Man stamps your ticket for eternal life.

Religion might have seemed like a bunch of rules and commandments while you grew up. As you get older though, you begin to understand that faith is more about a relationship. The same is true with family. My relationship with my parents is completely different now than it was growing up. I respect them, and they support me. There has always been love in the relationship, but now it takes on a different form.

Proverbs 1:7 explains it best: "The fear of the LORD is the beginning of knowledge; fools despise wisdom and instruction."

Respect, love, and an understanding that relationships are a process can help you as you relate to your parents now. As you continue to grow in your relationship with your heavenly Father, remember His commands, but more important, remember the love and obedience the Son showed for you on the cross.

Reflection

Your mother always will be your mother. Your father always will be your father. Your Father always was and always will be your Father. Same with your Brother, known to the world as Jesus.

Please do not separate yourself from your parents, even though you are "of age," as the law says. There is no curfew on parenthood. They remain your parents as long as they live. Not that parents should always treat you like you are fourteen or seven or two! As Aaron mentioned, your relationship with your parents is all about, well, relationships. Now you've reached a point in your life when it is time to enjoy your parent-child relationship as never before. It is a relationship guided by maturity at several levels, of give-and-take and of unconditional love.

Parents like to give advice. Most of the time, they give with the expectation that you will take it! Verbatim. Without too many questions.

Let your parents down gently.

Parental advice sometimes will be hard to take—or even bad to take. You are at the point in your life when you are able to make that decision. But what sometimes gets in the way is pride or a strong desire for independence—at the cost of wisdom or safety.

You are, as they say, "of age." You must exercise self-discipline to resist selfish or dangerous impulses. God grant you the strength to do that. God grant your parents the strength to accompany you appropriately through such struggles.

One of the most famous parents in all history was the father in Jesus' parable of the Prodigal Son (Luke 15:11–32). You may remember this account from your Sunday School days. Jesus told the story to illustrate a father's love despite a son's foolish decisions.

The son left home, having ample resources to live on his own, but exercised decisions that squandered his resources and threatened his future. The father was brokenhearted. Probably angry too, at times. But he never stopped loving his son and longing for the day when they might be reunited.

Given all the circumstances, most fathers would be sorely tempted to disown or distance themselves from such situations. But the story is not really about worldly dads. It is about the model dad of eternity—God Himself. And it is the story of how the divine Dad never stops loving His children, even when they defy sensible curfews. This Dad is perfect, far beyond the imperfections of earthly parents (who often need your forgiveness!).

Your heavenly Father placed a curfew on the devil. Curfew? More like a leash! While the devil continues to lie to you and drag you into a life of unrepentant sin, there are limits to what he can do, unless, of course, you prefer to stay in range. But your heavenly Father has pledged your safety—and your welcomed return when you stray.

Paul says it this way:

> For I am sure that neither death nor life, nor angels nor rulers, nor things present nor things to come, nor powers, nor height nor depth, nor anything else in all creation, will be able to separate us from the love of God in Christ Jesus our Lord. (Romans 8:38–39)

23

SANCTUARY

Hebrews 9:24–28

Do you ever feel trapped in an endless cycle of routines or circumstances? Perhaps the monotony of your days has just become unbearable? No matter what job or position you take, do you see it coming to an end because of your supervisor's personality? Are meaningful activities just not what they used to be? Do you desperately seek sanctuary?

You might be having an issue with vocation. Vocation includes meaningful work, a vision and a purpose, and the capability to do the job well. Have you given much thought to your vocation? What are some areas of life you are most passionate about? Do you enjoy certain activities or settings more than others? Is there something you feel called to do?

Through nudges from the Holy Spirit, God calls you to a vocation. Some have the vocation of son or daughter. Others may have a calling as an engineer or a church worker. God has crafted you to be a meaningful contributor in the world.

You may be in a holding pattern right now, possibly feeling trapped. You may even become disheartened by circumstances that repeatedly happen to you. But search for your vocation. Pray. Be open-minded to where God might want you and how He wants you to contribute. As a Christian, He wants you to share His Good News in all that you say and do.

The lesson here focuses on direction. Life has patterns. Think back to your college days. Even though every year was different, you still had a pattern. Imagine what life would be like without the comfort of a routine or pattern. Spontaneity has its place in life, but without patterns, life would be chaotic and hectic!

Your body responds to patterns too. If you consistently go to bed at a certain time, your body will start to prepare for sleep at that time. On the flip side, if you wake up during the week at 7 a.m., most likely you will be awake at 7 a.m. on Saturday and Sunday.

A pattern provides direction. You find securities and comforts as well as anxieties and discontents. If you are feeling hemmed in, it might be because your pattern is not consistent with the direction you want to head.

I have been trapped a few times by snowstorms. Roads shut down, electricity lost, and there is just a helpless feeling associated with really wanting to go somewhere but having to stay put. You know the direction you want to go but simply cannot safely head that way.

The priests of the Old Testament had to repeatedly make sacrifices on behalf of the people. Talk about a pattern that gets old fast! As a sinner, you struggle with the same entrapment of sin. Perhaps you can sympathize with Paul when he says, "For I do not do the good I want, but the evil I do not want is what I keep on doing" (Romans 7:19).

The repeated process gets old. But thankfully you have a Savior whose forgiveness also is never-ending. As Hebrews 9:26–28 says:

> For then He would have had to suffer repeatedly since the foundation of the world. But as it is, He has appeared once for all at the end of the ages to put away sin by the sacrifice of Himself. And just as it is appointed for man to die once, and after that comes judgment, so Christ, having been offered once to bear the sins of many, will appear a second time, not to deal with sin but to save those who are eagerly waiting for Him.

Live in the safe sanctuary Christ provides. Let Him lift you out of the dungeons of life and into the castle of His protection. Search for your vocation and be open to that vocation changing directions on you! Take heart in knowing that God never changes, and His love for you will always be shown in His sacrifice on the cross.

Reflection

You have many options in seeking sanctuary from personal and job-related routines. Some are helpful; others are harmful. And either can be sinful.

Think about that last sentence.

Among vocational and recreational alternatives are many opportunities that are potential "happy-makers." They appeal to your desire for sanctuary from whatever makes you unhappy or stressed. You know the truth though. Just because something makes you happy or relaxed, or otherwise appears helpful, does not mean that it is good. Things that are harmful need not work too hard to disguise themselves as helpful.

The most obvious culprits are alcohol, smoking, and drugs. Yes, yes, it is likely that you have heard this sermon before. But truisms will find their way to you with the same persistence of old wives' tales. You might not need warning, yet people who care about you will warn you often. Find sanctuary in the words of your faithful friends.

The Bible is the best place to find legitimate sanctuary. God, in grace and mercy, directed His early followers to reveal what He wanted us to know about Him. He knew we would find comfort in Scripture's many accounts of how God's people found sanctuary in His promises and His interventions. The trick is not waiting to find His comfort until you need it. Read randomly or select a reading plan from one of the many Bible websites available. What you read now will come back to you when you need it most!

One disclaimer is in order, though. Do not allow the helpful to become harmful. Obsessive reading—even of the Bible—serves more for the purpose of isolation rather than sanctuary. Some seemingly devoted and intelligent followers were even known to cloister themselves, to hide from life behind walls. In the end, they absorbed loads of knowledge and piles of piety, but they did little to share their sanctuary with others.

God allows you a lot of freedom. Wise believers choose to invite the Holy Spirit's guidance in their everyday decisions.

Prayer is another sanctuary. Talks to God—long or short—are helpful. And God talks back, usually not as voices in your head but as words in—you guessed it—the Bible. Through all of life's struggles—vocational, social, emotional, spiritual—you can take sanctuary in Jesus Christ. He lived and died for you, despite your bouts with harmful choices!

More important, He came back to life for you. His sanctuary never closes its doors.

24

Courage
Matthew 10:26–33

In his book *Eruption*, Mark Twain says, "It is curious that physical courage should be so common in the world, and moral courage so rare."

It is curious, Mark. When I first heard that quote I was blown away at the validity of this statement. Society puts strong emphasis on having physical courage. Moral courage is all but disappearing in the world—at least moral courage based on the Bible. Honorable courage in today's society includes applauding those who are born male but dress as females or standing outside of capital buildings with pro-abortion signs. Sure, it is courageous to be different or to have a different opinion, but where do those notions originate? For the ways of the world, those ideas come from selfishness or the consequences of bad decisions—that truth is found in one's self, in what you feel is right.

But that is not what the Bible says. Truth is only found in God's Word. You may believe something with the strength of Jericho's walls, but if your belief is not founded in Scripture, be ready for the consequences.

God provided the Law. He says what is right and what is wrong. Having courage to stand up for God's way is definitely a challenge in today's society. In Matthew, Jesus talks to His disciples about having courage in the face of persecution. Much like the time He sent out the seventy-two disciples, Jesus lets His followers know that life will not be easy. He tells His people to have courage, even though it may not be popular or easily understood.

My sister, Allison, is a shining example of moral courage. Four or five months into her first pregnancy, she had complications. The doctors discovered that the baby's brain was not forming correctly, and that was causing some other defects and problems. Life expectancy was very low. Even if the baby survived birth, she probably would live only a few hours.

Allison was told she had a few weeks to decide if she wanted to have an abortion.

I believe a life starts at conception and that this life was precious to God. She was a child that He loved, but if there was ever an "acceptable" time to have an abortion, it was now. I would not have judged my sister. I would not have abandoned her regardless of her decision. But she decided to carry little Johanna to full term.

The challenges she faced of showing up to work or Sunday worship must have been overwhelming at times. With friends breaking into tears or her students asking the "why" questions, it must have been unbearable for her to be out in public. The strength it took to continue on, to uphold God's Law even without understanding, took a lot of moral courage. Carrying her baby from the time of the news to her birth in January had to have been the hardest time—knowing that the life inside of you would be snuffed out quickly by the evil of this world.

But Allison endured. With the support of her husband, Paul, the two of them faced the inevitable on January 22, 2014. Baby Johanna lived for roughly four hours. In that short time, she experienced nothing but love! Surrounded by family, the sweet little baby girl was baptized and received into the arms of her loving Savior in the same day. Her mother's courage was a blessing to the lives she was able to touch in the short amount of time Johanna was alive.

We don't always understand God's will or comprehend why bad things like this happen. Even in the face of total confusion, God calls us to trust Him. He lays out His will in His Law and shows us His love in the Gospel. Even when we fail to do His will or make decisions contrary to His Law, He still loves us—a love that He showed in the sacrifice of His Son.

It takes courage to be a hero. It takes courage to stand up for what is right. Just be sure that "what is right" is also founded in Scripture. Jesus tells His disciples in Matthew 10:32–33, "So everyone who acknowledges me before men, I also will acknowledge before my Father who is in heaven, but whoever denies me before men, I also will deny before my Father who is in heaven." It takes courage to acknowledge God. That courage can take many forms, but the form that leaves a lasting impression is through your actions.

My sister's message is more powerful than 1,000 people praying outside of an abortion clinic. Her statement is more of testimony to what Christ has done for her, than a hundred news stories talking about transsexuals. God wants you to stand upon His Word even when the choice is not popular with what the world says. If you fail, know that He still loves you! And have courage!

Fourteen months after Johanna passed away, God blessed Allison and Paul with a beautiful and happy daughter, Olivia.

This lesson ends with God's promise to Joshua: "Be strong and courageous. Do not be frightened, and do not be dismayed, for the LORD your God is with you wherever you go" (Joshua 1:9).

Reflection

God the Father's Child died too. Grief-stricken family and friends mourned Him, though one is tempted to ask why because He told them He would live after death. Yes, even with that assurance, grief blanketed the mourners' spirits and faith.

You have the assurance of living with Jesus forever in heaven. What's more, history gives us a faith boost! You have the additional comfort of knowing Jesus has already died, risen again, and gone on to heaven ahead of us.

No doubt you have already faced a few situations with the courage only faith in our loving God provides. You certainly will face many more challenging situations, but you need not face them alone. Even now, form strong bonds with Christian friends who will support you through sorrow and danger. Pray for your family, and ask them to pray for you too—even, or maybe especially, in good times. They will be there for you when your needs increase.

Another need will arise when you must defend your faith. As Allison and Paul spoke of their faith in Jesus Christ before a doctor who had other beliefs, you may need to do the same. You may have to stand up for your faith before those who aggressively or seductively challenge your behavior. Some will wonder how someone as smart as you can believe in God as Creator. Others will question your stability or reasoning in believing the unbelievable story of what Jesus has done for you.

Have courage. Old Testament prophets refused to cringe before kings. Jesus stood firmly in doing His Father's will and endured terrible pain and unjust execution. Paul, the apostle, got beat up a lot. By now, you may be thinking that you do not want to experience anything like that. Have courage. The kings that terrify you may be a boss or a family bully, and people will likely use words instead of fists to beat you. Still, have courage because "the Lord your God is with you wherever you go" (Joshua 1:9).

25

Fish Fry

John 21:1–19

I will never forget the fishing trip to northern Wisconsin.

I was finally old enough to go up north with my uncle and my dad on an excursion of a lifetime! When we pulled out of the driveway in our green Chevy, I had no idea what the week would hold. I was familiar with shore fishing, as we went at least once a week in the summers, but I had never really been fishing from a boat. After a long summer of preparing for the trip, we were finally on our way!

The drive took longer than I had imagined. What in reality was only a five- or six-hour trip felt like I was in the car from sun-up to sun-down. The cottage in the woods was not as grand as I'd envisioned. Even with modern plumbing, a full kitchen, and most of the amenities of home, I still felt as if I was "roughing it." (No television!) The lake was beautiful and the surroundings spectacular. There were spiders as big as my face, frogs and toads almost everywhere we stepped, and pitch-black nights where we could see a sky filled with stars.

We had an awesome pontoon boat to fish from, a lake full of fish, and very few restrictions. After exploring the lake and locating some good fishing holes, we quickly figured out which lures worked and which ones the fish were probably laughing at. In a lake full of Perch, Northern Pike,

Muskie, and Walleye, I was in heaven! I was bringing in a Perch every three or four casts! My dad, on the other hand, was going for THE BIG ONE. The lures he used were about the size of the fish I was catching, and those Perch were not small! As my uncle and I reeled in fish after fish, my dad still insisted on going for the big one.

It was definitely fun catching all those fish, but I imagine one monster Muskie would have won the prize! Toward the end of our trip, we had a live well full of Perch. My uncle had caught the lone Walleye, and I had hooked an old Northern Pike. But my dad had not gotten his trophy. Still, the number of fish we caught was pretty respectable.

In preparations for our last dinner, my dad and uncle were expecting an amazing Perch fish fry! I, on the other hand, did something that I am fully ashamed of as I reminisce. I told them I did not want to kill all those fish and eat them. I do not remember much of an argument from either of them, but I know that my opinion was not the popular one. I was only a kid. My opinion should not have mattered that much. The meal would have been outstanding! But my dad and my uncle valued me more than a delicious meal. Their priority was my happiness, not their own self-indulgence. Their relationships with me were more important, and their selfless actions affirmed that priority.

Our society has a "priorities" problem.

Look at debt. Look at class distinctions. Look at Sunday mornings. As a youth leader, I often encounter problems with priorities. There are so many travel sports leagues and activities scheduled on Sunday mornings. There are options that take up entire weekends sitting on the lacrosse field, miserably watching the game!

I see families buying bags of Flamin' Hot Cheetos with their welfare money instead of milk, bread, and other staples for healthy nutrition. Others owe credit card companies thousands of dollars and yet still take lavish vacations. I am not completely innocent either when it comes to priority problems. As a sinner, I have the same problem Adam and Eve had—I think *my* way is best.

What does the Bible say about how you prioritize your life? Matthew 6:33 says, "But seek first the kingdom of God and His righteousness, and all these things will be added to you." Jesus told His disciples to make decisions based on what would bring glory to God. Ask yourself some questions the next time you need to make a decision: Do your actions bring glory to God? Do they point others to Him?

I often tell my students that God should not be on a list of priorities. When ranking the importance of family, school, work, and other values in life, God should not be number one. Instead, God should be the number one influencer for each of these areas. He influences your choices on the football field. His Word should guide your decisions at school and at work. The Spirit should be alive within your family and in your social life. God wants all of you all the time, not just a set amount of time each week. Your heavenly Father wants to have an effect on who you are and on all you do.

On the night when Jesus was arrested, Peter denied Jesus three times. At the time, Peter's priority was saving himself. After the resurrection, Peter and some other disciples were out fishing. They were getting skunked—not a fish in sight! Jesus appeared on the shore and told them to try a different spot. By simply fishing off the other side of the boat, they barely had the strength to haul in all the fish! When Peter realized it was Jesus on the shore, he no longer regarded his selfish priorities over his relationship with the Lord. Peter flung himself into the water! Jesus was once again Peter's first priority. He could have drowned. He could have helped his friends haul in the fish. He could have waited until the boat reached the shore. Instead, Peter couldn't wait to hug Jesus.

The rest of the details in John 21 still amaze me! There were 153 large fish (v.11), and Jesus had breakfast with the disciples. (I am glad the child version of me was not there—I probably would have told the disciples and Jesus to let the fish go!) The conversation focused on Peter as Jesus three times asks, "Simon, son of John, do you love Me more than these?" Jesus then says, "Feed My lambs. . . . Tend My sheep. . . . Feed My sheep." (John 21:15–17)

Simon Peter affirmed his love for Jesus. He would not deny Him again, even in the face of his gruesome death.

Take the plunge with Peter. Get out of that boat!

Reflection

I never caught THE BIG ONE.

I was so intent on catching the big one that I caught very few smaller ones. My priority prevented me from the sheer joy of fishing. That happens sometimes when your priorities are out of whack with reality.

You might be tempted to look only for dramatic spiritual events in your life. Maybe it is something like convincing a Muslim friend to learn more about Jesus. Maybe it is healing you of some disability or addiction. Maybe it is comforting a dying uncle that Jesus loves him and that they will indeed be together soon. And the uncle whispers something about seeing Jesus as he breathes his last. Something big! Something amazing!

You might have an experience like that, but do not miss opportunities for the little things—prayer, kind words, godly concern for those in need, gratitude for all the small blessings from God.

Go fishing. God will give you the catch you need. Do not throw any of them back!

26

Relma Johanna Charlotte Doering Vanick Eick

John 13:1–20

My grandma had six parts to her legal name! She was a complicated woman, full of wisdom and memorable sayings. I had a close relationship to my Gram, as she picked me up every day after school, and we spent a lot of time together. We ran across the street every day and grabbed a milkshake from Portillo's for $1.68. I counted out the correct change from her change purse, and we complained together whenever the price increased.

Relma had many life experiences. She survived the Great Depression, endured scarlet fever, and underwent the loss of two husbands. She taught me a lot. Many of her sayings helped me endure hard times. She often said, "Kill 'em with kindness" and "Treat others the way you want to be treated." Other learnings were subtler and came from shared experiences, such as: "Do not make cream of chicken soup with eggnog" and "Watch out for cracks when pushing someone in a wheelchair!"

Family was the most important *thing* in her life. With every ounce of love she possessed, she loved every child, every grandchild, brother, cousin, niece, nephew, in-law, and everyone related in some way. She even loved her friends as if they were family. I did not know *Aunt Lil* was not an actual aunt until I was in my teens!

She modeled her faith well, finding ways to let her light shine. She served her congregation by polishing pews and sharpening pencils. She had a servant attitude—no work was ever beneath her. She never served begrudgingly, ever eager to serve the Lord. As her abilities diminished after a few falls and some heart problems, she still continued to iron and dust, making sure to do what she could. She served all the way to her last breath.

One of the most impressionable memories she left behind was her humming. She always hummed songs such as "What a Friend We Have in Jesus" or "Go, My Children, with My Blessing." Her relationship with God was very strong. She modeled an exemplary faith life to anyone who spent any amount of time with her.

Who is a role model for you? Who has helped shape your faith?

In John 13, Jesus demonstrates the ultimate example of servanthood when He washes the disciples' feet. As He willingly and lovingly shows humility to His followers, He teaches a lesson that could only be learned through experience. He taught many lessons by being a role model to the disciples.

Have you been a role model for someone?

God puts people in your life to set an example of faith and service. Some people can model their relationships with God without effort! For others it takes a little more consciousness.

Relma impacted those around her. Jesus changed the lives of those around Him. He empowers you to do the same. His love and sacrifice changed your life. You are no longer bound to the consequences of sin but free to live differently. You can leave a legacy with those around you, not to bring praise to *your* name but to bring glory to the Father.

May your relationships with others be influenced by heroes of the faith, including those you know personally. May you serve those you encounter as Jesus served those He encountered. May those you meet remember you for your faith-filled attitude and actions.

Reflection

Relma was indeed one of Aaron's role models. He did not mention the times they clashed. He usually lost those battles of wills, being no match for the persistence and convictions of his grandmother. And that was a good thing! If role models are true role models, they stand with confidence in the face of resistance or rebellion.

Jesus was that way. He was kind and forthright, gentle and firm, merciful and corrective. He never gave in to foolish whims, His wisdom exceeding political correctness or indulgent capitulation. Jesus was the perfect role model.

Many role models do not consciously decide to be role models. You will not find classes or books on how to excel at role modeling. Role models tend to come by this gift naturally. This is not to say that role models avoid conscious decisions about their behaviors; they may think about how they act and who they are in terms of influence on others.

Role models mostly model the Law side of things: how to act, how to converse, how to make decisions, what to do in difficult situations—all aspects of moral, social, and ethical behavior.

The risk involved in modeling proper behavior is that role models will slip into impropriety—even sinful impropriety—on occasion, sometimes even often. But role models have an additional responsibility—perhaps the most important behavior—to model repentance. You cannot look to Jesus as a model there—He never needed forgiveness; He preached the need for it (Mark 1:15). Repentance can be difficult because it involves swallowing pride or admitting guilt. Both feel bad but do good! And they are good characteristics for role models to exhibit.

The additional element of repentance is changing sinful behavior. You probably know how hard that is. Some role models might be accused of hypocrisy here, when the real culprit is weakness—a characteristic of all role models whether or not they realize it. Sometimes the best you can do is to hate sin!

Role models model forgiveness—that which they receive and that which they extend to others. Jesus was the ultimate model here. He forgives because He loves us, and He died to take away our sins. You can forgive because He first forgave you—and now you have both the power and the obligation pay it forward and forgive others as you have been forgiven.

You may not have six parts to your legal name, but then again maybe you do if you add Christian, Repentant Sinner, Saved . . . Though those names do not appear in your signature, they most certainly do in your life.

27

Counting Sheep

Genesis 37

When I was in high school, I experienced some spooky, almost "prophetic" dreams. There was the time my friend's sister was in a car accident the day after I had a dream in which it happened. Then there was the dream about messing up in a concert. That sure made me practice! I also have to mention the many times dreams helped me see the situation I was in more clearly. I have always been a dreamer, and I remember dreams well.

Remembering dreams is not always a blessing. I also remember nightmares very well. As a child I had many recurring nightmares. There were the times I could not overcome Power Rangers monsters, and other times I was riding a single-rail, incomplete roller coaster over Lake Michigan.

The most memorable recurring nightmare I remember involved a monumental point in my dreaming career. After having enough of the nightmare, I finally took over and acted consciously in my dreams. The villain in my dream was Ursula from *The Little Mermaid*. She has the upper body of a woman and the lower body of an octopus. Her silver hair and black tentacles are the stuff nightmares are made of. In these dreams, seven of my friends along with me were seated in a circle, one at the end of each of her tentacles. A different colored Crayola marker that somehow doubled as a single-shot gun was in front of each of us. For weeks, I went for the marker/gun, but she would grab me before I was able to stop her. I remember in one dream she turned the gun on me, and I actually woke up coughing with the taste of smoke in my mouth! But Ursula could not hold me captive forever. One night, with a cue toward my friends, we distracted her, and I was able to grab the marker and end the dream.

I never had that dream again.

You can psychoanalyze me all you want, or you might simply say I've watched too much television, but dreaming has been and always will be important to me. It is prevalent in the Bible and can be an inspiration in life.

Look at Joseph in Genesis 37. His dreams implied he would have power over his brothers. With already strained relationships with him, his brothers "hated him even more" (v. 8). In place of killing him, they sold him into slavery. As a result, Joseph fulfilled God's plan through a position of power among the Egyptians.

Dreaming can be inspiration for life, but sharing dreams at the wrong times can cause problems. Take Joseph for example. When he told his dreams to his brothers they were in the midst of a power struggle. They already did not like him much, and even his father rebuked him because of his dreams. On the other hand, Joseph interpreted a dream at a timely moment for Pharaoh and was restored to a high position. Timing and situation are important.

You really do not have much control over your dreams. You do not decide when you dream or what you dream about. Sometimes you can influence your dreams or plan your sleep patterns, but you still have little control of your dreams. What you can control is how and when you accomplish your dreams.

Beyond the dreams of your sleep, what are your dreams in life? I am sure Joseph never dreamed about what he was capable of doing when his brothers traded him. What are you capable of doing? How do your dreams challenge you?

God gave you an amazing brain and an ability to dream. Dreams are terrific when they bring glory to His name and foster an environment of grace. Sadly, you are bound to the reality of sin. Maybe your dream job feels like it will never come. Maybe you feel as if you will never meet the person of your dreams. The longer you wait for your dreams to come true, the harder it is to believe they will happen. Sin loves to tell you your dreams will never happen. Satan loves to lie and tell you heaven is just a dream.

Do not listen!

Instead, look to God's promises. He promises to be with you always (Matthew 28:20). He promises nothing can separate you from His love (Romans 8:38–39). He promises when you seek Him, He will give you the desires of your heart (Psalm 37:4).

God wants you to dream, and He wants you to have goals. He wants your inspiration to coincide with His will and assist His kingdom in coming. He wants you to be a part of His plan for all people to come to a knowledge of the truth (1 Timothy 2:4).

Reflection

I once saw Davey Crockett outside my window. He was leaning against the porch railing. I knew it was Davey because he was wearing a coonskin cap with the tags from The Alamo Gift Shop still attached. Besides, I had just seen him on television. Who could mistake him?

My mother.

She mistook him for a figment of my imagination and took more control of my viewing habits, which was not difficult in those days, there being only four channels.

Dreams pique the interest of theologians, oneirologists, and just plain common folk like you and me.

Theologians, naturally, explore the dreams of prophets and others, mostly in the Old Testament, rather than the television-, diet-, or sleep-induced phenomena. Jacob's ladder dream (Genesis 28:10–17), for example, was not the result of an illicit late-night ham salad sandwich or a lumpy pillow. God sent him the dream, laced with a generous promise and blessed assurance. God did not limit this particular communication style to those in the Old Testament. Peter, Paul, John, and others heard from God in this way too. Does God talk to you this way? Don't count on it. He has already revealed all you need to know in the Bible.

Oneirologists look at dreams from the machinations of the mind. Dreams take the form of premonitions, altered states of consciousness, or thoughts most on one's mind. You might have some of these—but they are not the works of God.

As for people like you, Aaron, and me, dreams come with sleep. When we remember them, our dreams have varied impacts on our lives. Sometimes they are sour, sometimes sweet. The characters may be villains, friends, or even White Christmases. But if you dream of a Savior, be assured He is real and not a dream. He came. He conquered. He waits for you.

28

Get in Line, God
1 Corinthians 10:13–14

> No temptation has overtaken you that is not common to man. God is faithful, and he will not let you be tempted beyond your ability, but with the temptation he will also provide the way of escape, that you may be able to endure it. Therefore, my beloved, flee from idolatry. (1 Corinthians 10:13–14)

The First Commandment must be the most frequently broken commandment. Idols are typically seen as other gods such as Buddha or the Hindu god Shiva. Sometimes idols are identified as money or materialism, a football team, or even sleep. Have you ever thought of an addition as being an idol? Do you know some of your addictions?

Many people are addicted to technology or social media. Other people have addictions to fashion or sex. Some fall into uncommon addictions including pleasure, power, and status. Still others fall into the more commonly recognized addictions of drugs and alcohol.

If you charted the amount of time spent on your activities of the day, what would it look like? Is your time centered on things God wants you to do, or are you bound to things that only matter on earth? Are you spending more time in Scripture and prayer than on Facebook or texting? Is your mind filled with ideas on how to best serve your neighbors, or is your focus on how to exploit them and get ahead?

God wants all of you; He wants you completely invested in Him. You have a relationship with Him. For a relationship to be healthy, there must faithfulness. Infidelity can be physical, emotional, or both. The intimate connection of two people during an affair is a clear disregard of the original relationship. If something is getting in the way of your relationship with God, take notice and get as far away from it as possible!

Look at Paul's first letter to the Corinthians. God empowers them by giving them permission to say *no*! God gives a way out from all temptation.

Oftentimes, the biggest reason for falling into a temptation or being unfaithful is you. Your sinful nature desires to get in the way of your relationship with God. The devil wants your relationship destroyed and wants you to convince others to cut ties with the Savior. Satan attempts to tempt Jesus with pleasure, power, and status (Matthew 4), but Jesus sees through the lies and overcomes the temptations.

Nothing the devil offers is worth severing ties with Jesus. I often compare this to a *Star Wars* example. Emperor Palpatine tells Anakin Skywalker that he can save his precious Padmé. All he must do is learn the ways of the Dark Side. Skywalker turns. Padmé dies. The Emperor is a liar, and the galaxy is doomed.

The devil is cunning and disguises the idols he uses to tempt you as appealing and desirable—even necessary—but they cannot fulfill their empty promises.

Only God is faithful. There may not always seem like a way out of temptation, but it does exist. It might be as simple as saying no, or it might be as complicated as changing habits to avoid situations in which you continually fail. Whatever the escape might be, rely on God. Trust in His promises. When you fail, repent. Turn from your sinful ways. Don't cut in line so that God is behind you. Let Him lead you, and be a faithful follower. Not only is God faithful, but He also loves you and forgives you. His promises are not lies!

Reflection

The idols most effective at drawing in followers are those disguised as benevolent or benign. No God-fearing Christian would ever carve a piece of wood or sculpt a chunk of metal and pray to it or trust it for guidance. Reading the account of the Golden Calf (Exodus 32), Christians wonder how anyone could be duped by a statue. But Satan knows that too. Age-old idols include anything or anyone considered more important than God—even if only for a moment (First Commandment).

Wow! The list would be endless. It would include many of the same items and people on the benevolent and benign list. Satan cleverly uses God's good things for evil purposes. Again, anyone or anything considered more important than God qualifies as an idol. Clearly, idolatry is more a corruption of the mind and soul than a person or physical object.

Some idols even appear Christian! One of the saddest involves praying to saints. You need not be so fearful of talking directly to God that you pray instead to Mary or any of the patron saints. God wants to hear from you. He sent Jesus to break down barriers between you and Him. Remember the story of how the temple curtain ripped apart when Jesus died on the cross? (Mark 15:38). That curtain symbolized the holiness of God compared to the sinfulness of His people. Only the High Priest could go behind the curtain to present sacrifices. Jesus was your High Priest; He brought down the curtain. You have direct access to God.

Church leaders sometimes become another of the saddest idols within Christianity. God's people sometimes equate pastors or other church workers with Jesus Himself. Have you heard the stories of trusting (but not scripturally discerning) people who follow their pastor into illegal or unethical activities, even suicides? When God indicates in His Word that something is wrong, you cannot equivocate. To do otherwise is to create an idol.

Now for what may be the hardest truth about idols—you.

Aaron hinted about this earlier when he said that all sins involve idolatry. Implicit in this is the fact that anytime you break a commandment, you are choosing your own will and volition above God's will and wisdom. Uh, that makes you your own idol. In other words, you make yourself a god.

You have lots of company. Since all believers are also sinners, all are guilty of idolizing themselves. Society promotes the process with its pervasive emphasis on self. Humanistic psychology has become the bible for educational and social philosophy and practice. Whatever feels right or rational becomes the standard that replaces the Commandments.

All idols eventually crash and burn.

St. Christopher icons have cracked and splintered in terrible automobile accidents. Corrupt pastors are prosecuted amidst reports and insinuations hurtful to good church leaders and followers. People discover the truth about their selves and live with disappointment, bitterness, and even self-destructive behaviors. And the saddest truth is saved for those who devote themselves to the non-Christian world religions. When they crash and burn, they do so literally.

You are not like them, even amidst the truths of your own self-centeredness. Jesus died and rose to take away your sins. He was the only one who could do that. Do you believe that? Then you are in the right line.

29

Life Jackets

Proverbs 3:5–8

"Trust in Lord with all your heart, and do not lean on your own understanding" (Proverbs 3:5).

It was a beautiful morning. I survived my first night camping with some college buddies, and we geared up for a canoe trip. I am not a strong swimmer—if you can even call what I do swimming—and I had never been in a canoe before. Sounds like a great combination, right?

Divided into two canoes, the five of us were ready for an adventure. Typical canoes have two benches, and since I was the amateur, I got stuck sitting in the bottom of the middle of one of the canoes. Tim and Dave—the thrill-seekers—were with me. Tony and Drew were in the other canoe with a cooler. To this day, I wish I had been in the other canoe!

The start of our journey was uneventful. The weather was nice, the current fairly slow, and exciting scenery decorated the banks of the mighty Fox River. As our journey progressed, I became annoyed with sitting in a puddle of water. They all sat on their life jackets to make the journey more comfortable, but I would not take off my life jacket. Again, they all knew how to swim.

Our trek down the river included stops on various islands, a friendship with a dying mouse, and running aground a few times in the shallows.

As we progressed, clouds started to roll in, and a little drizzle fell on us, turning our excitement into misery. Not having been on that route before, no one knew how far we had gone or how much paddling remained.

We "raced" the other canoe at times, aiming for the slight rapids in the water and getting a small boost of speed. Tim and Dave were determined to reach the end first. But becoming fatigued (or just lazy), my canoe crew started to fall behind. Up ahead, we noticed our "power-up." A rapid much bigger than any we had seen so far would be our next opportunity to gain momentum. (Please understand my term *rapid* probably falls on the negative side of the class scale of rapids.) Tony and Drew noticed it too and went for it. As they passed by, they shouted, "Don't do it!"

It was too late. We, too, were committed.

Arriving closer, we noticed why they warned us. On the left was a gigantic underwater boulder, the top just skimming the surface. About three feet to the right was a full-size fallen tree, parallel with the current. Somehow, Tony and Drew made it through. We did not. To avoid the boulder, we drifted right and became lodged against the fallen tree.

After an exaggerated push-off, we freed ourselves, but our push-off turned us backward. We attempted to remedy our situation but ultimately ended up perpendicular to the flow of the water.

On that day, I learned a canoeing lesson: never get sideways in the water!

Our canoe was t-boned by a tree stump, and we were dumped into the water. I have never been more grateful for taking safety precautions. My whole body submerged momentarily, but then the life jacket did what it was designed to do. This story ends in a ten-minute battle of us fighting the current to free our canoe from the tree and a half hour of a very angry me snuffing out any more "fun." Needless to say, the next year I was in Tony's canoe.

I like to think the life jacket saved me. In all reality, my friends would not have let me drown, and, honestly, the river was shallow enough that all I really had to do was stand up.

But life preservers are designed to save lives. They wrap around your upper body and keep your head above water to prevent you from drowning. They are not always comfortable, and they might feel unnecessary, but you need one most at those unexpected times.

A life jacket is like Jesus. He wraps His arms around you—arms that He spread on the cross. He prevents you from drowning in your sin. There may be times when you feel you do not need Him or other times when His Word is not comfortable. It might be unattractive to have Him draped across your shoulders, or you might even think you can "swim" just fine by yourself.

Don't try to paddle through life on your own.

As the proverb states, "Do not lean on your own understanding." Trust in God. A life preserver is designed to be a lifesaver. Jesus was sent to be the Savior of your eternal life.

No matter what you are going through right now, whether it is an enjoyable float or a capsized canoe, let God's love wrap around you and keep your head above water.

Reflection

"Wear your life jacket" always outranked "bon voyage" whenever anyone in our family (mostly Aaron and I) left for an outing. We heard it at least three times, not including the cell phone reminders from our loved ones who remained on dry land.

We took their advice seriously—and compliantly. Although, I harbored the fantasy that if the ship—err, boat—went down, I could sink to the bottom and run for shore. And the truly rebellious side of me wanted to claim biblical authority for not wearing a life jacket, Peter being the prime example (Matthew 14:29); but that kind of justification does not hold much water, so to speak.

Venturing out on the water without a flotation device makes no more sense than venturing out in life without Jesus—as Peter discovered (Matthew 14:30).

What does it mean to let God's love wrap around you? What sounds easy in words can be difficult in real-life situations. Even though the "moral" of Peter's story encourages us, the reality of being in sinking situations comes upon us suddenly and often without warning. But Peter did the right thing—after he did the wrong thing.

Peter cried out to Jesus, "Save me!" He didn't stop to fold his hands and formulate a formal prayer. He did not wait for a lull in the thunder to be heard. He didn't waste time pondering his error and wondering if Jesus would listen to him despite his lapse in faith. No, Peter was in trouble and did not hesitate to cry for help.

Hearing Peter's story, the temptation is to focus on Peter's momentary faith flaw. I like to focus on his quick recovery from the error. The Holy Spirit planted sufficient faith for Peter to quickly recognize the source of his salvation.

Life has its ebbs and tides. Sometimes you walk through them, other times you sink into them. Ask God to be your life jacket during both times. And always be ready to cry to the only Friend who can save you. In fact, your salvation already is *fact*, no matter what happens on earth.

30

Anger

Ephesians 4:26–32

Anger is not sinful in itself; even Jesus became angry (Mark 3:5). Anger becomes sinful through the response to anger or in the situations that follow. Revenge and bitterness can easily erupt over a situation that starts with anger. Much more difficult is showing self-control or letting go of the hurt that someone may have caused.

You will become angry—and that in itself is not bad, but be careful as anger is an open door for the devil. As Paul's words to the Ephesians say, "Be angry and do not sin; do not let the sun go down on your anger, and give no opportunity to the devil" (4:26–27). Paul's message here has three parts:

Part One

"Be angry and do not sin." How did Jesus do it? If you look at the account in Mark 3, you see that Jesus was angry at the Pharisees' actions. These were people who should have known better and should have been actively showing love to those in need. Jesus was angry not with them as people but with their sinful behaviors. He loved even the Pharisees but was grieved by their lack of faith.

Even while overturning tables in the temple, Jesus did not sin. Jesus exhibited self-control even in His anger. I am sure the people in the temple were not happy with Jesus, but He behaved with righteous anger toward the injustice He witnessed. He drove out the animals and moneychangers, but no one was hurt. Once again, the house of worship was returned to an atmosphere of purity and holiness.

When you become angry with someone, analyze yourself. Why are you angry? Is there a selfishness attached to this anger? Are you angry at the person or at their sinful behavior? How are you acting upon your anger? Is your anger controlling you, or are you controlling your anger?

Part Two

"Do not let the sun go down on your anger." Jesus does not remain bitter over any of these situations. His anger diminishes, and He does not hold grudges. No bitterness remains in His heart.

Paul's message is "do not stay angry!" Anger can easily take control and affect all your actions. Be sure to deal with anger properly and in a timely manner. Grudges and bitterness can permeate your actions and affect your relationships. Anger not properly dealt with can hurt you and others around you.

Create a practice of working through your anger. Do you deal with your anger in a timely way? Are you able to let go and forgive others? Do you obey God in spite of your feelings and emotions?

Part Three

"Give no opportunity to the devil." The devil has enough opportunities. Anger puts the ball on the tee. The devil wants nothing more than for you to disobey God, and he uses anger as a club—a club that hurts you and others. Use the power of the Spirit found in God's Word to snuff out anger, don't let it consume you.

Take a deep breath next time you become angry. Ask yourself whether your actions glorify God or open a door for the devil. Remember, the devil cannot control your actions even when you are angry. Through the Holy

Spirit you still have the power to deny the temptation of revenge or of holding grudges.

Self-control is difficult when dealing with fallen people. It helps to remember you are a fallen person too. But even in your failures, God loves you. He showed you this love in the person of Jesus. Even in His pain and torment, He loved sinners.

Paul sums it all up in his letter to the faithful in Ephesus, "Be kind to one another, tenderhearted, forgiving one another, as God in Christ forgave you" (Ephesians 4:32).

Reflection

Ah, Aaron delivers a lecture worthy of any preacher, teacher, or parent. But do not be angry with him. He speaks the truth, and truth often hurts. And even if it does not hurt, truth can be hard.

Have God's truths made you angry? Are you disgusted by Old Testament accounts of God's instructions to utterly destroy enemy nations—men, women, and children (Numbers 21:2–3; Joshua 6:21)? If this is the first you have heard of this, I hope the shock does not drive you away from God. God had good reason for His commands. The Canaanites were ungodly and mortal enemies of the children of Israel. They were fierce obstacles standing in the way of the land God promised to His children.

How about the opening chapters of the Bible, when God banishes Adam and Eve from the Garden of Eden—after only one sin! (Which you, by the way, inherited from them.) Then God even placed an armed guard—an angel with fiery sword, no less—at the garden's entrance so the two cast-offs could not sneak back in. Where is God's love here? Upon serious analysis, if the couple had returned to the garden and eaten from the Tree of Life, they would have lived forever in sin and misery instead of going to heaven—a new garden from God.

Jesus spoke many hard things. Some believers shrink at the candid harshness as Jesus told people there was only one way to heaven—belief in Him. They might shudder to think that Jesus called His enemies a brood of vipers or that He told disciple Peter, "Get behind me, Satan" (Matthew 16:23). Was Jesus really this angry?

What angered Jesus most were lies—lies proclaimed by the devil and his followers or insidiously planted in the minds and hearts of people wanting a culture devoid of God and His holy will. Their lies would be fatal to believers tempted to believe them. How harsh might you sound while warning a child not to run across a six-lane interstate?

Are you angry that God calls you a sinner?

Human nature rebels against wrong, especially when accused of it! Teachers in Christian schools tell stories about parents who have become livid because teachers have told their children they are sinners. Some churches are popular and growing because those who attend never hear the hard truth about their sinful nature. They miss the love behind the message.

You cannot know you are saved unless you know your need to be saved. The Holy Spirit wanted God's children to know this vital fact of life, so its truth appears in the Bible. You might think of it as the original bad news/good news situation.

The bad news is that you were born a sinner—your sin inherited from Adam and Eve—and you commit many sins of your own, even though you are a Christian.

The good news is *the* Good News: Jesus lived, died, and rose from the dead to deliver you from your sins—to take them away, leaving you with the promise of living forever with Adam and Eve as your neighbors.

Now *that* fact makes Satan angry.

31

Selfishness or Investments?

Matthew 25:14–30

Squirrels populate almost every location in the United States—and quite possibly most of the world. Squirrels come in many colors, sizes, and abilities. Lots of squirrels visit my front yard. One of their most frequent behaviors is to dig holes and bury their food. One of my least favorite behaviors is pulling out the growth that is a result from whatever they had buried.

I never see a squirrel return to dig up his plunder. Maybe my dog Harvey does since he sits in the window all day, but he doesn't usually tell me about it. Instead, I discover shelled peanuts in the middle of the yard after the snow melts. You know . . . all those "native-to-Michigan," lightly salted, shelled peanuts!

I have often wondered why squirrels store away their treats. They must have a basic instinct to save up for a rainy day or a period of drought. Or maybe they are just selfish. Rather than let their squirrel brethren enjoy that delicious cashew, they hoard it under a layer of grass.

Thinking about selfish squirrels brings up the topic of saving. It is important to save. Having an emergency fund or an account to fall back on in case of job loss is vital. It is important in today's society to always have back-up plans. But is it biblical?

I think that answer rests in the intention of saving. Why do you want to save money?

In the Parable of the Talents (Matthew 25:14–30), Jesus tells about three men receiving talents. In biblical times, a talent was the heaviest monetary unit of weight. Each of the workers does something different with the talents the boss gives them. The first doubled the amount through trading. The second also went and made double the amount entrusted to him. The third, however, dug a hole and buried it in the ground. (Luckily he was not a squirrel and remembered where he buried it!)

He was afraid.

Assuming things about his master, the third servant put himself in a state of worry and concern. The other two servants intended to benefit their master, and the master rewards each as he instructs them to "enter into the joy of your master" (v. 21).

Are you saving to hoard or to invest in the kingdom of God? Note one important thing about your money: it is not yours; it belongs to God. Everything we have comes from the hand our loving God. Are you wisely making use of the money with which He blesses you, or are you frivolously squandering it? Are you like servants one and two, or more like the squirrelly servant?

Where is your focus? Matthew 6:21 reminds us, "For where your treasure is, there your heart will be also." Squirrels put their treasure in the ground. They forget about it. It has no value to them once they selfishly hide it away.

Our basset hound, Ivy, is a stubborn, hard-to-train dog. She is excessively possessive, defensive, and territorial. Even though she is two years old, she has to stay in her kennel if we are not around. Harvey spent only a few days in the kitchen behind a gate before he could be trusted in the house. Ivy cannot even be trusted gated up in the bathroom. Our two canines remind me of the words of Jesus in Luke 16:10: "One who is faithful in a very little is also faithful in much, and one who is dishonest in a very little is also dishonest in much." What has God entrusted to you? How long a "leash" do you have? To keep Ivy sane and a contributing member of the household, we have to keep her leash short. She needs discipline and structure. Financial health is closely related. Spending and saving both need to be disciplined and structured, but again it goes back to intent.

Who are you serving? Yourself? Others? God?

God blesses you to be His servant in this world. He gifts you to serve others. You belong to God. You are a priceless treasure, paid for with the blood of the Lamb. Trust Him to provide your daily bread, and use what He has given you to point others to Him. If your heart dwells on spreading the Word of God and sharing His love with those around you, then you will have treasure enough to do so!

Reflection

Negativity about squirrels runs in the family. Aaron sees them as stubborn and selfish. I see them as gluttons, highly favored by the bird food industry for their contribution to bottom line profits.

Do not put out a bird feeder unless you like birds more than you dislike squirrels or if you have stock in a bird food company. Do not put out a bird feeder unless your aim with a softball is better than a squirrel's ability to dodge it (and your neighbor's toleration of your idiosyncrasy and the sound of a softball banging against his house).

Okay, so this is not about squirrels. It is about you.

And it is not about bird seed or nuts. It is about blessings.

God gives many gifts, some of which we appreciate, some of which we treasure, some of which we ignore, and some of which we squander. As Aaron asked, "What do you do with yours?"

Oh, did I say *yours*? I meant to say *His.* God just lets you use what He gives you, much like the boss and the workers in today's Bible reading. This parable puts a godly spin on blessings and their uses.

If your blessings include a high-paying job, then use some of your reward to support Gospel mission work or godly charities. If your blessings *do not* include a high-paying job, use some of your reward to support Gospel mission work or godly charities.

If your blessings include talents in the fine arts or carpentry or competent driving or smiling or in any way that can bless others, go for it. Your blessings need not be spectacular or even bountiful. God blesses you to be a blessing to others.

If after reading this you are puzzled as how to best use your inventory of blessings, be patient—and be alert. God provides opportunities.

And one more thing: God blessed you with His grace and mercy. He blessed you with a Brother, who bore the punishment for your sins. God forgave you for Jesus' sake and now invests the Holy Spirit's power in you to tell everyone what Jesus has done—for you and for them.

32

Finding Community

Philippians 2:1–11

In high school, I played drums in a garage band called Grant Street. We played at a few church picnics and lock-ins and possibly even a talent show or two, but most of the time we just jammed. As the drummer, I never thought twice about loading the drum set and transporting it to wherever we played. (I did so every Saturday for worship anyway.) We did not really have a genre. We covered Bob Dylan, The Strokes, The Killers, and even a Radiohead song. About five or six songs were originals. It was a fun time!

The rest of high school was not much of a fun time. I struggled to find a sense of community. I was on the golf and tennis teams, in the Wind Ensemble and Jazz Band, and also in a few academic groups. Even being super involved, I struggled to find my niche, my place to fit in and actually feel part of the community. Even in Grant St. I felt like the outsider.

Growing up (and even into high school), I found community at St. Paul Church. Congregation members knew me, I participated in worship and youth group, and I always felt welcome. My family was a major contributor to the life of the church, and that environment fostered community. That changed over time, as I prepared to enter college.

I found my next community at Concordia University. This Christian community was supportive and provided many opportunities for me to live out my faith. My immediate community was formed freshmen year and involved two friends who are still my closest friends to this day. While we started out as three complete strangers, we ended up eating lunch together for the next four years. College also provided other community opportunities: The Wind Symphony, Cougar Tennis, and LEA. Many of the friendships I formed in those groups have turned into life-long relationships.

Since graduating, my concept of community has changed. There will never be another opportunity for the tight-knit community I was part of in college. Perhaps you are realizing that too. God created humans to be in community with others. So now that you are out of college, where do you fulfill your need?

I have only found community in a few places since college. First is family. Family is one community you are born into and cannot change. Family changes when people get married, when loved ones die, and when babies are born, but your family community remains fairly constant. The second place I consistently find community is in the Church. Being a professional church worker can make it difficult and complicated to find community within my congregation, but it still is the starting point. In both central Illinois and west Michigan, I have a valuable group of other DCEs and church workers who make up a strong and supportive network of friends.

The last place of consistent community is with life-long friends, relationships developed over the years. You may not see these friends often, but when you do it feels like only a few days have passed.

Where do you find your community, now that you are done with college? Have you found a local congregation yet? Are you becoming an active part of that faith community?

Community only lasts through genuine and authentic relationships. Love and care must be apparent! Love and care are fostered through humility and strengthened by living life together. Consider this lesson from Philippians 2:1–11:

> So if there is any encouragement in Christ, any comfort from love, any participation in the Spirit, any affection and sympathy, complete my joy by being of the

> same mind, having the same love, being in full accord and of one mind. Do nothing from selfish ambition or conceit, but in humility count others more significant than yourselves. Let each of you look not only to his own interests, but also to the interests of others. Have this mind among yourselves, which is yours in Christ Jesus, who, though He was in the form of God, did not count equality with God a thing to be grasped, but emptied Himself, by taking the form of a servant, being born in the likeness of men. And being found in human form, He humbled Himself by becoming obedient to the point of death, even death on a cross. Therefore God has highly exalted Him and bestowed on Him the name that is above every name, so that at the name of Jesus every knee should bow, in heaven and on earth and under the earth, and every tongue confess that Jesus Christ is Lord, to the glory of God the Father.

Reflection

God sent His Son away to school, so to speak. Did you catch that in the Bible words above? God "emptied Himself, by taking the form of a servant . . . in the likeness of men." But the Son did not leave home to learn. He left to live like a human, teach, and die like a criminal.

Why would God do such a thing? The reason also is in the passage above. God was polite enough not to say it this way, but I will: God knew we would not "get it." Centuries passed with God's children misunderstanding God and His promises. They never seemed to understand that the Promised Land and its King were intangible.

Oh, God did lead them to a physical Promised Land, a place well short of the heavenly Promised Land but a good place to live and call their own, a place in which generations could pass until Jesus, their Savior, was born. Old Testament records tell the story of how God's children resisted, rebelled, and feared along the way. God taught through the prophets, but His children were often unreceptive and disobedient learners.

Finding and practicing community fared no better in New Testament days. One would think the people who waited so long for the Savior would accept Him when He arrived. But even His closest disciples often did not "get it." Their confusion about Jesus' kingdom persisted—right alongside their learning from the Master Teacher.

Only after Jesus died and rose did a more solid community develop. Most members of the community did not come from the former faith community—the community that sought to kill Jesus in the name of God!

Jesus' ragtag Early Christian Church was led by the apostles, among them His closest disciples from a variety of vocations, plus a few others—including a former mortal enemy, Paul. Jesus and the apostles made it clear to new believers that the community of Christians was open to all people. The Early Christian Church was the first to not discriminate on the basis of race, ethnicity, sex, color, or anything else. His Church—His community of believers—was open to all who professed faith in Him as their Savior.

You are now part of the long-standing—the everlasting—community of faith known as the Church. Pray that the Holy Spirit makes you an active member of that community. This is no time to sit back and enjoy the privileges of membership. Those privileges do not exist on earth, even though you can celebrate your membership. And while you celebrate, why not invite others to join you?

33

Love Abounds

1 John 4:7–8

My mother is very loving. She often shows love through gift giving. Every time I visit, I leave with a grocery bag full of my favorites from stores not found in Michigan or little items she has picked up from farmers' markets and other locations she frequents. Andie has learned to be careful in admiring things when we are stores with my mom because whatever she admires usually ends up as presents from my mom. She is extremely generous and caring.

I have learned a lot about love from my parents. Even the few times I was spanked, I learned about love. Of course, it sure didn't seem like love at the time, but even those occasions taught me love is not simply a feeling that comes and goes. Rather, love is a commitment. It is a constant state of putting the other person's needs before your own. My parents are shining examples of this truth.

The love my wife and I share was tested immediately after we got married. Her parents sent us to Hawaii for our honeymoon. We had a fantastic time there, immersed in God's beauty. We definitely saw a glimpse of paradise. But after doing many of the touristy things and trying to pack our time full of fun, it was time to go home.

We arrived at the airport in the evening since we had an overnight flight to Phoenix before connecting to Chicago. It was quiet in the airport. Most of the little convenience stores were closed already. The night before, we attended a luau where I tried sushi for the first time. The next morning, before our departure, we went snorkeling at Hanauma Bay. By that evening, we were exhausted as we sat in the quiet airport and waited for our plane.

During our wait, I started to feel a little sick. Knowing the plane was going to board any minute, I rushed to the bathroom to try and gain some composure. Instead of finding peace and motivation to get on the flight, I threw up! I hadn't really felt that bad. Hoping it was just a fluke, I grabbed a Sprite from the only open store and boarded the plane.

It was not a fluke! Before take-off and all through the night, every ten minutes, I threw up. I do not know how I survived. The flight attendants did not have any medicine to help, and the medicine I was taking was not doing a thing. I truly believe I was sitting next to an angel on the plane. The patient man in the aisle seat next to me graciously moved every ten minutes throughout the night.

When we landed in Phoenix, I was very weak. I could not walk on my own and definitely was not strong enough to navigate the airport. Andie ran off, bought some crackers and medicine, and quickly brought them back. Again, they did not work. Using her as a crutch, I made it to our connecting gate and onto the next plane. Once again, there was someone in the aisle seat next to me, but he quickly vanished after take-off. The flight from Phoenix to Chicago was just a shorter version of the flight before.

I would have kissed the ground in Chicago if I thought I could have gotten back up! I was diagnosed with traveler's sickness after a quick trip to urgent care. Andie drove us home the next morning. Once we'd arrived home, she immediately came down with the same symptoms. Our first few days back home as a married couple were definitely spent "in sickness," not "in health."

I share that story because I am not a very lovable person when I am sick. I am a baby, and I complain incessantly. Andie's commitment to love me remained beyond her feelings for a sad, pathetic wretch.

I was sick a lot as a kid, suffering from ear infections every other month or so. My mom taught me the meaning of love through those times of sickness. Her commitment to me (again, as much of a baby as I was) showed that love exceeds emotion.

You have a sickness too. The sickness is sin. You cannot overcome that sickness on your own. You need something more to help you. The cure comes from Jesus. His blood is not simply medicine; it is the cure. Through His death and resurrection, we see the result of sin and a glimpse of the cure to come in eternity.

John tells us, "Beloved, let us love one another, for love is from God, and whoever loves has been born of God and knows God. Anyone who does not love does not know God, because God is love" (1 John 4:7–8).

If you replace the word *love* in that passage with "commit to put the needs of others before our own," you begin to understand God's love a little better.

Mark 12:30–31 gives us the Great Commandment: Love (be fully committed to) God and love others (put their needs before your own). This simple but challenging lesson is best learned through experience. Thank God for all those who love you and have loved you. Ask God to help you become a better lover of Him and of those around you.

Reflection

Love is a much used and abused word. Aside from the scriptural definitions Aaron cited, love can be applied to toys, shows, wine, beer, cars, liver sausage, and almost anything else. Some use love synonymously with sex or as a term of endearment or as a tennis score. (Whoops. Where did that come from?)

On the more positive side, love is something parents, children, relatives, friends, and pets do. Love is best when it is mutual. One-sided love and love lost result in broken hearts and fractured relationships.

As Aaron mentioned, no love is greater than the love of God, through Jesus Christ, who even died to save those He loved. His love prompts us to return that love, to both Him and others.

Uh-oh. You see the glitch here, right? Sometimes our love relationship is one-sided or lost. Love fails with sin, especially if you think of each sin as another agonizing nail on the cross. You may even (I pray not!) experience a time when you lose your love for Jesus. Satan is glad to assist you in that department.

Good thing Jesus' love *is* one-sided! Jesus loves you always, even—maybe especially—at times when you do not love yourself—when you are sin-sick, wretched because you cannot find relief for your guilt. Jesus is the only cure. Your prescription plan will not cover it, but a little song can help. Sing or hum or whistle if you cannot remember the words, "Jesus loves me, this I know . . ."

The Bible does indeed tell you so.

34

Entertaining Angels

Hebrews 13:1–2

"Let brotherly love continue. Do not neglect to show hospitality to strangers, for thereby some have entertained angels unawares" (Hebrews 13:1–2).

Have you entertained angels? Perhaps you were "unawares." I believe there were two times in my life when I encountered angels.

Chicago was just a fifteen-minute train ride away from where I went to college. My friends and I would hop on the train to spend weekend afternoons downtown. There are many homeless people and beggars in the city, but none like the woman my group encountered one day.

She was outside of a Potbelly's, and, surprisingly, there was no one else around. It must have been a Sunday because many places were closing down, and we had some urgency as we headed to the "L" station to catch the last train out.

As we raced past Potbelly's, the woman said, "Good evening beautiful people. Could you help me buy a sandwich for my meal today? All I need is three dollars and sixteen cents." In our haste, we quickly replied with "sorry, no change" or some other generic answer.

Her reply is what was so different than usual responses. She said, "OK, well thank you so much for acknowledging me. You folks have a wonderful evening."

Something made me look back toward her as we headed up the steps to the station, but she was not there. I paused and looked every direction she could have gone, including into the restaurant.

She was gone.

I believe I failed at "entertaining an angel" that day. I will never forget her or the kindness in her response compared to my selfishness.

And then there is the second time I believe I encountered an angel. I like to spend time in coffee houses. A diverse group of people enjoy coffee or the treats offered by such places. One day, I saw a young man enter the building. The man was wearing jersey shorts and a hoodie and looked like he had been walking for a while. It was an awful day to be outside. It was one of those classic Michigan days when it was rain one minute and snow the next, with a constant wind howling from the northwest. The drenched man approached the counter and ordered a small coffee. At this particular place, the small coffee is not exactly the smallest size coffee you can get. The "small" is twelve ounces, and there is another cup that is eight or ten ounces (extra small?).

The small (twelve-ounce) coffee rang up at two dollars exact. The man started rustling through his pockets and started to look frazzled. He found a dollar but could not find the difference. He asked if there was a smaller size, and the barista displayed the extra small cup and said, "Yes, this one is $1.79."

The man felt around again hoping to find a few quarters that he may have missed the first time. No such luck. Embarrassed, he apologized and went to use the restroom. The cashier apologized as well and returned the dollar he had given her.

Again, the situation just seemed to have an unusual feel as I watched it all unfold. This man was obviously not having a good day. When I bought my drink an hour earlier, I noticed that I had two dollars left in my wallet. The Holy Spirit encouraged me to get out of my seat, go up to the counter, and tell the barista to give this guy a coffee when he came out of the restroom.

The people behind the counter were shocked, but the barista took my two dollars. When the man came out of the bathroom, the employee stopped him and said, "Sir, here is a cup for your coffee."

"But I did not have enough money to pay for it," he replied.

"Don't worry about it, someone else paid for you."

"No, really, I didn't have enough. It's okay."

"But sir, you don't understand. It has been paid for. It is yours!"

The man was speechless. He filled up his cup gratefully and continued on his journey. This man, like the lady before, also seemed to vanish into thin air.

Jesus did the same thing for you. You do not have *enough* to cover the cost of your sins. Thankfully, your debt has been paid, and your sins have been forgiven! The verse from Hebrews reminds us to show love to our neighbor, to practice hospitality. Through serving and loving your neighbor, you just might be entertaining angels in disguise. The lesson here? Practice hospitality. Serve your neighbors and show love to your neighbors—even those who might not seem to be worth your time or your two dollars.

Have the same attitude as Jesus Christ who took the form of a servant and humbled Himself, even to the point of death (Philippians 2:7–8). You belong to God. He has redeemed you. Share that freedom He gives you with those who need a little love.

Reflection

I think I once entertained a bad angel. He confronted me outside a restaurant in Chinatown after my (wiser) family members had already gone inside while I parked the car. He was quite the hustler as he asked me just enough questions to make it seem like he had seen me somewhere. He needed "a few bucks to, you know, get back to his car at that gas station in town, you know . . ." I had a "few bucks." But not for long. My family had observed the man from the restaurant window as he approached several other people. He was confident. Familiar. Just the kind of person you might want to help. Unlike myself, the others were not fooled.

Hustlers and the needy exist side-by-side. In some ways, both are needy. Erring on the humane side normally harms nothing more than ego.

For me, the key word in today's passage is *entertain*. Entertaining is fun and provides the entertainers as much satisfaction and reward as the person being entertained.

Did you sense the good feeling in Aaron's account of the coffee house incident? Have you experienced anything similar? Doing something good and helpful to others has made you happy too, right?

Jesus loved you—once a stranger to Him—enough to give His life for you. That was the work He came to do, and it was not just to make Himself feel good. He loved you. Okay, so you read that a few words ago, but they are words that you never tire of hearing.

Next time you encounter an "angel" who needs entertaining, you might find it difficult to discern true need. Ask the Spirit to guide you. Just add it to your entertainment budget.

35

Useless Information

1 Kings 3:1–15

I never really liked school. I always excelled with little effort, except when it came to tests. Tests were often a struggle, even after many hours of studying, but I still managed to keep A's in my classes. Most days, I raced ahead during class to finish my homework before I left for home so I could have time to play Ninja Turtles or watch a White Sox game. My philosophy became work first so I can play later.

Things did not change much in high school. I dreaded the half-hour drive in the morning and couldn't wait until the afternoon bell rang. For the first time, though, I had to put some effort into maintaining straight A's. Math seemed to be the most troubling subject for me. I could arrive at the right answers, but could not show my work properly. This became especially apparent during AP Calculus—the class that had me working backward from my correct answers to show how I arrived there. Praise God that when I took the AP Calculus test, I received a 3 and never again needed to take another math class!

College did offer me challenges and workloads that had me struggling late into the nights. Unlike the previous thirteen years, I finally started to enjoy classes and was challenged by the opportunities.

When Andie told me she was going back to grad school, I thought she was crazy. She had just finished her undergrad. Why would anyone want to endure the punishment of two more years of school? Do not get me wrong, I am not against learning, but the classes and homework take forever! Trying to balance school with family, work, and church can just create a flurry of busyness.

Looking back, my biggest problem with school was the amount of useless information. Learning a Robert Frost poem or hearing about Custer's Last Stand (for the fortieth time!) just did not spark any excitement. Why? I will never use a Robert Frost poem or talk about Custer's Last Stand—other than in this writing—ever again. There was too much emphasis on knowledge, and not enough focus on wisdom. I view wisdom as knowledge you use.

As I moved away from the conventional model of formal education, I have found learning to be high on my priority list. I want to know Scripture and be able to reference a passage without looking it up on Google. I also need to know about the students I teach—who they are and how they best learn. Math comes in handy for budgeting purposes, as well as setting preschool tuition or planning a servant event trip.

I spend my learning time reading books that others more knowledgeable than me have written. Often I have to remember that just because something appears in a book does not make it true. The Bible is the only book that contains complete and always reliable truth.

In Solomon's prayer (1 Kings 3:1–15), he asks God for wisdom. More specifically, he asks for an "understanding mind . . . to discern between good and evil" (v. 9). It was a bold request, and God fulfilled it! But look again at how Solomon views himself in verse 9. He says, "Give your *servant* . . ." A servant's role is to follow instruction and get the job done. Servants always must be ready to learn new tasks and how to better perform their duties to keep their masters happy. Lifelong learning is definitely a priority for servants.

If grad school is on the docket for you, great. I pray the process goes very well and that you gain much knowledge and wisdom on your journey. If you are more like me, done with school, do not give up on learning, especially in the area of Scripture. God's Word is filled with background information, context, and wisdom. Pray the prayer of Solomon: that you would have an understanding mind ready to discern good and evil. You will impact those around you, and God will use you to further His kingdom.

Reflection

Like Aaron after me, I attended a Christian elementary and high school. They were good places that tried hard to meet the needs of every student. Like Aaron, I did not consider school among my favorite activities. Math was a terror. I may be the only person in the world who has advanced degrees without ever taking geometry. (I fulfilled math hours with lower-level classes.) Oh, I hope that revelation does not result in subjecting my diplomas to recall.

Useless information sometimes becomes less useless as you age. You see the wisdom of learning fractions when you buy lunchmeat, though I suppose fractions have many more important functions. History becomes more enlightening when you perceive how the past has contributed to the good, bad, and ugly today. And science becomes an astonishing delight when you place it within a scriptural worldview!

Scripture may seem full of useless information to readers who are not wearing their faith glasses. Like the poor third grader who cannot see the math problem on the board because the numbers are fuzzy or the struggling first grader who cannot read because the words are blurry, you cannot make sense of Scripture without help.

Faith is like a pair of glasses that helps you to see strings of words as strings of God's words. Approaching Scripture with willingness to learn can overcome skepticism—an "I don't believe this stuff; convince me" attitude. Not that an open attitude is a prerequisite to consuming, reading, and understanding God's Word. The Word has power to penetrate hard hearts and hard heads.

Paul was the Christian's worst nightmare. He was a learned student of Old Testament Scripture. He did not consider Jesus' teachings simply useless. He considered them blasphemy. But Jesus wanted Paul on His side. Paul was no match for the Holy Spirit, who literally knocked him off his "high horse," fitted him with faith glasses, and sent him on dangerous missions to preach the Gospel (Acts 9:1–19).

Paul did not go from highly educated to highly faithful in one easy step. He had a teacher who, by the power of the Spirit working through Scripture, taught him the truth about Jesus, his Savior.

Too often, people think of the Old Testament as, well, old! But more than a collection of stories that take up Sunday School time or that might even make a good movie, the Old Testament tells the story of how God never abandoned His people, sinners as they were, and how He—over centuries of travail and threat—kept alive the promise of a Savior.

As you read Scripture, marvel at God's plan for you. When you find Scripture a bit fuzzy, get help. Check out a reliable and scholarly resource such as *The Lutheran Study Bible*.* Remember some scholarly resources are more like Paul in his early years, seeking to poke holes or cast doubts on Scripture. Seek out reliable resources that truly study and explore the truth of the Scriptures.

God bless you as you learn more about your Savior, Jesus Christ.

*No, this is not a boldfaced advertisement forced by the publisher but a sincere endorsement of *The Lutheran Study Bible* as a good book of the Good Book.

36

Forgiveness
Matthew 18:21–22

The best definition I have heard of forgiveness comes from a book by James Hunter called *The Servant*. In the book, Hunter compares forgiveness to giving up resentment. Forgiveness is not always an easy thing to give. The word *resentment* is powerful. Resentment is not part of my daily vocabulary; however, feelings of resentment often have influenced my attitude and actions.

Who has wronged you? Toward whom might you be feeling resentment?

In the Lord's Prayer, we ask to be forgiven as we forgive. Numerous times, Jesus pushes the issue of forgiveness: the prodigal son (Luke 15), the woman caught in the act of adultery (John 8), the unforgiving servant (Matthew 18), and, His best example, straight from the cross (Luke 23).

Jesus was definitely wronged. He did nothing worthy of the punishment He received; however, He did not resent those who crucified Him. In fact, He prayed that they would receive forgiveness because they did not know what they were doing. (Think about that the next time somebody cuts you off in traffic!)

Let's dig a little deeper on what forgiveness is and is not. Forgiveness is not denial. Forgiveness is a clean slate. Forgiveness is not an invitation to the same sin. Forgiveness is removing bitterness or grudges from relationships. Forgiveness is not conditional. Forgiveness is a response to the love we receive from God. Forgiveness is not optional. Forgiveness is a command.

While teaching Peter and the other disciples about forgiveness, Jesus made it clear that there is no limit on the number of times to forgive (Matthew 18:21–22). The implication is that it does not matter if the other person is sorry or going to change his or her ways (repentance); God still commands forgiveness.

What does it really mean to give up your right to resentment, to truly forgive?

There are no worse feelings than those that result from guilt—of being so sorrowful, so penitent, and so conscience-stricken because you have wronged someone. Guilt happens when you realize you have wronged someone and you see no apparent way to fix the relationship. In that type of situation, the person who has been wronged has all the power. They have the power to forgive or to condemn. True reconciliation may never come. It is a result of the fall—Eve and Adam's disobedience of God. Forgiveness is the first step toward restoration.

Sin has consequences. Forgiveness can have powerful consequences too. Jesus' example from the cross saved one of the thieves who was dying alongside Him. When you forgive others, you extend Christ's forgiveness and extend that forgiveness out of your life and into the lives of others. When you forgive others, you are fighting sin and the evil that it brings. When you forgive others, you are obeying God's command and showing a complete reversal of how the world says you should respond.

We respond to Christ's great sacrifice by forgiving others. Give up your resentments toward those who have wronged you—do not retaliate or hold grudges. Through your example, you reflect Christ's forgiveness. When you are on the other side of forgiveness, do not let guilt drive you to despair. Jesus paid the price for sin on the cross with His blood. Live in that promise and live in His love and forgiveness.

Reflection

What will most people answer when asked the most distinguishing characteristic of a Christian?

Many will say that Christians are good people. They are kind, considerate, and do not use bad language except maybe when some idiot cuts them off on the interstate. Whoops. Sorry about that. But therein is the problem with that definition. Christians are not always kind, considerate, or especially exempt from using bad words.

Some will answer the question with statements about faithful church attendance, Bible class participation, or service on a church board or committee. All those are good things, worthy marks of an active Christian, as long as individuals resist the urge to boast about their goodness. The Bible has harsh words for such people (Luke 18:9–14).

Do you classify yourself a Christian? How would you describe yourself within that classification?

Suspecting a trap and noticing the title of this piece, you may create an answer that has something to do with forgiveness. And you may be right.

Christians are forgiving people. Aaron made that clear and encouraged you toward that end. If you are exceptionally good at forgiving, you also are talented at forgetting.

Yes, forgetting presents a problem. If it is any consolation, God is the only one with unblemished expertise at forgetting. Things you long remember and regret about yourself have no place in God's memory. He is perfectly forgetful. Whew!

You, on the other hand, have a better memory of sins—your own and the sins of others—than you have of where you left your car keys or cell phone. One of sin's consequences is the (or "an") inability to forget. One of grace's consequences is the ability to not allow bitterness or self-recrimination to accompany the memories of sin. While forgiveness always is a benchmark of Christians, the best way to talk about it springs from what God does rather than what Christians do. Your ability to forgive would have no consequences had God not initiated the action for your benefit (Colossians 3:12–13).

The true marks of a Christian? Others will notice yours. And their occasional absence. But you will never go wrong if you boast of the one thing that's always accurate: "I am forgiven. Jesus takes care of me."

Footnote on Forgiveness

Satan uses some sins of the past to plague sinners with guilt. It happened to Judas, who likely thought his betrayal unforgivable. Please never say "I cannot forgive myself" or "I'm too terrible for God to forgive." The devil pleasures himself by planting those thoughts in your mind. God has experience with billions of incidents—forgiven and forgotten. He will do the same for you.

37

The Back of a Squad Car

Psalm 91:11–15

Have you ever called 9-1-1? I never did until my internship, and I probably should have had them on speed dial. After the first time I called, it seemed like I contacted them every three or four months!

A few times, I was the first observer of an accident, so I called them in. Another time, there was a dead deer in the middle of the road, and a bystander begged me to call and report it—weird situation! There were also a few falls at church that I had to call in and request help.

The most memorable 9-1-1 call occurred on a night of sheer terror. The area in which I lived was not the worst of neighborhoods, but it also was not the best. I had witnessed a few car break-ins in the carport beneath my bedroom window, as well as a domestic dispute (both times I called 9-1-1). It should not have surprised me when I woke up in the middle of the night to a persistent pounding sound. This noise was different than the frisky neighbors downstairs or the loud footsteps of the neighbor above me. I looked out my window and noticed the absence of their cars, so the source of the noise had to be coming from somewhere else.

I glanced toward the outside security door and noticed someone's shoulder. Attempting to get a better view, I groggily walked over to my apartment door and peered through the peephole, which had a perfect view of the security door. My heart began to race as I saw the rest of "the shoulder."

It belonged to a good-size man who was ramming his other shoulder into the Plexiglas door. The man had to have been at it for a good minute or so before the integrity of the door was compromised. The entire sheet of Plexiglas flew into the stairwell. I hurriedly grabbed my cell phone and called for help. On my way back to the door I grabbed the Louisville Slugger from my bedroom closet. Panicked and afraid, I whispered to the dispatcher what the problem was, but my voice was all the indication needed to share that I was in danger.

I peered through the peephole and watched as the burly man stumbled to the upstairs apartment. He pounded on the door many times. Time seemed to slow, and it took forever for the police to arrive. The pounding stopped, and I could hear footsteps staggering back down the steps. I watched nervously through the tiny peephole as he went right past my door and stopped. Instead of pounding on my door, he started to relieve himself. Obviously, the man was drunk. But he did not leave, and I noticed the shadow coming toward me. As I stood back and quieted my voice even more, the pounding started.

There I stood—phone in one hand, baseball bat in the other. I had it planned that if the lock gave out and the intruder came through the door, I would drop the phone and swing for a homerun.

Thankfully, the deadbolt held, and the dispatcher said the officers had arrived. I did not hear any sirens or see anything, but amazingly the intruder vanished. I ran to the front of my apartment and heard some shouting. It was the officers with their flashlights and radios. I threw open the balcony door and identified myself as the caller. They asked me if I got a good look at the man, and I confirmed that he was about a foot away from me, on the other side of a wooden door. (They also asked me to drop the baseball bat.)

They told me to stay put and wait for them to come back. Five tense minutes later, they arrived and told me they found two intoxicated men down the street. They asked if I would be willing to identify the one who broke in, and I agreed.

The back of the cruiser was pretty tight. The plastic seats felt like I was sitting at a child's picnic table rather than in a vehicle. My legs were folded up to my chest—and I am short; it was very difficult to not slide around back there. The officer gunned it down the street and pulled into a parking lot. There was the culprit, in handcuffs, standing against another cruiser. As the officer's spotlight made contact with him, I confirmed that it was indeed the man who broke in.

When I returned home, the maintenance man was replacing the Plexiglas, and I turned on a movie and made some coffee, as there was no chance of falling back to sleep!

The 9-1-1 number is the well-known "help hotline." As a child, you are taught to call that number in times of emergency, when you need to contact the police or fire department. But how do you contact God? Since there is not a Psalm 911, look at Psalm 91:11–15.

I would much rather have an angel sent from God than a baseball bat and a cell phone. God is there. He is your protector. In verse 15, He promises, "When he calls to me, I will answer him; I will be with him in trouble; I will rescue him and honor him."

God promises to always "pick up." More important, the communication lines with God are always open and active. The 9-1-1 dispatchers are a reliable earthly blessing. God is even more reliable and will always respond to your calls for help. Unlike times in which you may have to call 9-1-1, do not just call to God in times of emergency. Rather, make your prayer life a daily routine, a conscious part of your day, and a continuous conversation with God. Take a lesson from Martin Luther: "Pray, praise, and give thanks."

Reflection

I was only in the back seat of a squad car once. I started out in a taxi at the time, which was at four o'clock in the morning, but my cab driver fell asleep and rear-ended a police car less than a block away from Chicago's main police station. In all the years I lived in the city, I had never seen so many squad cars show up as quickly as they did that morning. That experience reminds me of the passage Aaron chose for this devotion. Like Aaron, I am glad God uses angels instead of police officers. Where is a police officer when you need one? Usually out of sight but reliably close by. Where is an angel when you need one? Always out of sight, and while God can send legions of angels, usually one will do.

Do you believe God has angels? The Bible talks about them regularly. God provides them many roles. Many of them are warriors.

You see, a war rages beyond your perception. The devil and evil angels try to take you, but God's angels fight to keep you. The spiritual warfare is fierce. You did not know you were such a prize, right? You are God's prize because He sent Jesus to take away your sins and take you to heaven. The devil prizes you because you belong to Jesus. Praise God for His angels.

Does all this sound so much like science fiction? Put down this book! Turn to Ephesians 6:11–12. Then look at Psalm 91:11–16. Read it and thank God that angels are more than knickknacks.

P.S. If you want an exciting story about angels, check out 2 Kings 6:8–23.

38

HOME FOR THE HOLIDAYS

Philippians 1:3–11

My family opens presents on Christmas Eve. Growing up, I thought everyone did. Once I got older I realized we were in the minority. Our family tradition on Christmas Eve was to go to worship, drive around and see Christmas lights (maybe even those in downtown Chicago), and then go home, turn on Christmas music, and exchange presents. One by one we would take turns opening presents until all of them were opened. On Christmas Day, we would wake up, go to worship, and then have a big Christmas dinner.

Those traditions changed my first year out of college.

I had to work on Christmas Eve, so I did not arrive at home until 11 p.m. I do not recall if we still opened presents that night. I just remember the celebration of the holiday seemed rushed and was less about Jesus and more about family. The next year was even harder because Gram went to meet her Savior just a week before Christmas. The few years following just cemented the fact that Christmas would never be the same as it was growing up.

Missing out the first year was definitely a misery. I had never missed a Thanksgiving or Christmas with my family. I had always been able to sit around the big table, thankful at Thanksgiving and joyous at Christmas as we celebrated the birth of Jesus. Family was especially important at these times.

Have you had to miss a celebration with your family? Have you felt a little alone during a birthday or on the Fourth of July? Does life just seem less enjoyable than it was as a child?

The Bible does not say much on the topic of homesickness, but Paul's desire to be with other Christians is close. In the opening statements of his letter to the Philippians (vv. 7–8), he writes:

> It is right for me to feel this way about you all, because I hold you in my heart, for you are all partakers with me of grace, both in my imprisonment and in the defense and confirmation of the gospel. For God is my witness, how I yearn for you all with the affection of Christ Jesus.

Paul's longing to be with the church he started is evident in the text. His explanation indicates they were family to him—brothers and sisters in Christ, fellow "partakers of grace." Paul's love extends beyond bloodlines. My first Christmas Eve away was spent with my church family. I felt welcomed and loved, but it was less satisfying than the warmth of being home.

Families change. People pass away, and babies are born. Others marry into the family, and still others are "honorary" members. Yearning to be with family and craving the comforts of the past are normal. Your family is dealing with a different perspective on these times as well. (I will let my dad speak about that one.)

Cherish and celebrate the times you do have with those you love, as well as create new traditions and memories. Family is an important part of celebrating holidays, but remember to focus on the reasons for the days. Because of Christmas and Easter, we get to partake in a homecoming of all believers, the homecoming we will celebrate for all eternity!

Reflection

Our family's perspective on "home for the holidays" reflects the warmth and riches of close family ties. Long distances and job responsibilities make get-togethers challenging, and memories of holidays past threaten our appreciation of holidays present and future.

No more do I tremble at the prospect of one of Aunt Olga's sloshy kisses or worry that cousin Finny will get to the eggnog ahead of me. No more wiping the steam from the kitchen window, hoping to see my sister drive up from out of town. No more waiting for the telephone to ring, bringing greetings from Uncle Bill and Aunt Mill, too old to travel but sharing their love anyway.

Yes, not having to celebrate holidays separated by locations and families would bring pleasure. And for the ones having to choose which holiday to celebrate where and keep it all balanced, well, what a relief if something better were possible. Realities are what they are. And we cannot let them dim the joy and truth of the events we celebrate.

Christmas is still Christmas—the birth of Jesus. New Year's is still New Year's—a time to remind ourselves that God is in our future, no matter what happens. Look behind other family gatherings and you can find similar affirmations for other events.

What are your memories? Depending on your age, you may not have as many as Aaron and our family, but I would guess they are just as powerful. To intensify feelings, songs of the seasons often introduce sentimentality. "I'll Be Home for Christmas," sung during war years, ends with the line ". . . if only in my dreams."

Federal holidays, such as the Fourth of July, resound with patriotic music, which might also prompt tears from families separated by never-ending hot spots around the world—and their deadly consequences.

If your holiday memories do not conjure pleasant scenes, you are less susceptible to longing for the past. I feel sad for what you have missed. I would not give up our past despite disappointing schedules and fewer loved ones together to celebrate.

Enough sentimentality! *Home for the holidays* is a worldly phrase right now. But a new day is coming. A new home too, for that matter. Jesus will come again to take us home for an eternal holiday.

The thought of Jesus' return frightens some. We whom Jesus has saved are not frightened. Maybe mildly anxious, to be honest, but not fearful. Our destination is known and certain. We are going to heaven. Schedules, tensions, history, weather, the economy, age, sloshy kisses—nothing will stop us.

See you there! Wait until you meet Aunt Olga!

39

Experience Needed

Romans 8:14–17

Your most recent interview ended just like the last one: "Sorry, we are looking for someone with a little more experience."

So why did you take so many classes to help certify you when employers are looking for nothing more than experience? How are you supposed to gain any experience if no one lets you acquire that experience? Your résumé means little if your job history is not impressive. This paradox is frustrating.

Success in so many areas of life ends up being who you know, not what you know. People become qualified more on the basis of relationships than on documented credentials. In an employer's mind, experience means capability. "Fresh out of college" employees will make mistakes, take time to train, and might not be reliable. To an employer, a rookie is a risk, unless someone can vouch for you.

But isn't the same true in terms of faith? The importance is not on what you know, but on who you know—or rather, who knows you. Romans 8:14–17 names God as Abba—Father. It lists you as an heir of God and a co-heir with Jesus. The term *heir* is not prevalent in today's culture.

Typically, inheritance is a passing on of property or possessions within a family, from parents to children. The one receiving the inheritance is an heir. What is the inheritance you, a child of God, receive from the Father?

Eternal life.

One of my favorite Bible characters is the thief on the cross who confesses Jesus as Lord. There is no biblical evidence to support the thief knew anything about Jesus. By witnessing Jesus' attitude and actions on the cross, the thief realized this man was something more. Jesus assures him *today* he would be with Him in paradise. For this thief, what he knew did not matter, but Who he knew became his salvation—he, too, became an heir of salvation. What a great gift of grace! Your salvation depends not on what you do, but on Who you know and what He did for you.

So what about that diploma of yours?

Well, continue your attempts to break into your field but be open to the opportunities God presents to you. Sometimes that takes a servant's heart. Sometimes the experience you gain will be in an unexpected area. Leave a legacy wherever you go. Be an employee who benefits the company and builds the company up. Be a co-worker who models the love of Christ.

Next, continue to network. Congregations are filled with people in many different fields of work. A job is not guaranteed, but perhaps a mentor/mentee relationship develops, and you receive a different kind of experience.

Praise God we do not need to go through the same experience Jesus went through. His suffering and death was more than enough experience required for us to become co-heirs with Him. I look forward to enjoying my eternal inheritance with you and with our amazing Savior!

Reflection

The interview for my first position went something like this:

"Where do you want to go?

"Anywhere."

"What do you want to do?"

"Anything."

I got the job. The placement people sent this northerner to a school in the Deep South to serve as a teacher in a double-grade classroom and as a principal to provide administrative help to another school that did not have their own principal.

I thought I could do the job well. Talk about inexperience! Or maybe I was just stupid. When a desperate employer cannot afford the cream of the crop, they must settle for a little sour milk. Epilogue: God taught both the congregation and me *a lot* through our experiences during my two years there.

Your Christian vocation actually begins with all the experience you need, not to be confused with all the experience you want. You already have faith, God's blessed gift purchased by Christ's sacrifice and delivered directly to you by the Holy Spirit. You begin, therefore, knowing and possessing the blessings of your Savior. This is the most vital element of your experience as a Christian. You need no additional experience to share this fact of faith.

Get more experience anyway.

No great sage needs to reveal the mystery of getting experience. You get more by doing more. It follows, then, that the more you read the Bible, the more experience you have with God's Word. The more you pray, the more you become comfortable talking to God and listening to His answers, which normally appear in God's Word. The more you share your faith, witnessing becomes easier, especially as you read about the powerful witnesses who came before you, as reported in God's Word.

With very little experience, you can detect a theme here. God's Word is an essential element in gaining experience.

Avoid one mistake in gaining experience: do not attempt it alone. You see, the more experience one has, the more tempting it is to become overconfident or self-sufficient. The experience may drive you to curtail obtaining more experience, thinking you have already experienced enough to . . . to . . . to . . . quit while you are ahead and not tangle yourself in a bunch of words. (You get the idea.)

God has called you to a purpose. Whatever job or career you are growing in now, the purpose is the same. You already have some experience with Ephesians 2:10, but repetition builds experience: "For we are His workmanship, created in Christ Jesus for good works, which God prepared beforehand, that we should walk in them."

Experience makes any job easier, but that does not result in an easier life. Glitches, even in repetitive tasks, call on past experience to inform corrective or adaptive reactions—and acquiring new and more useful experience. The apostle Paul is a good example of this.

Paul was an experienced traveler, walking and sailing mostly. His missionary travels required some additional skills, and so he gained experience in surviving beatings in hostile locales and shipwrecks. Through it all, Paul's purpose never changed. Directed by God and filled with experience, he wrote Ephesians 2:10.

May your faith and life experiences ever be Spirit-filled and lead you never to be satisfied with the experiences you already have.

40

Perception vs. Reality

Romans 5:8

The topic of change came up at the beginning of this book. Change can be difficult, but it also might be necessary. Before we change too much, let me ask a few questions. What is your reality? Debt? Job struggles? Loneliness? Are you truly happy? Do you find satisfaction in how you spend your time outside of work? Is your spiritual life thriving? These might be hard questions to answer, but the answers themselves might be even harder to accept. Is your perception lining up with your reality?

I think it safe to say that everyone wants to be successful. Everyone wants to be happy. But not everyone is happy. That is simply reality. Perhaps you know an unhappy person, or perhaps you are unhappy. Again, it can be a normal part of life, and coming to terms with reality can be difficult, but often it is necessary in order to excel in life.

So is your perception of happiness also reality in your life?

Andie and I were visiting a remote hop farm on a comfortable spring afternoon. The farm also had a couple horses and other livestock. There was a brewer's conference going on, so a bunch of people were just wandering around the farm taking in the rural sights and sounds. Two fenced-in horses were in front of our parked car. I do not spend a lot of time around horses, so this seemed like a unique opportunity to pet a horse. I called the horse to me with some clicks and whistles and hand gestures, and, amazingly, it worked. Andie warned me that the fence surrounding the horses looked like an electric fence. I disagreed as the cables were coated in plastic, and it was logical to me that plastic is a poor conductor of electricity. To prove my point, I tapped on the wires with the back of my hand.

Nothing happened.

The horse came over and I started to gently pet her snout as I stuck my hand between the two wires. She did not like where I was petting her, and she started to push her snout up, moving my entire arm. Part of that process caused my arm to lift the top wire . . .

After a loud snap, crackle, and pop, I quickly learned how this electric fence worked.

The electricity traveled through my arm into the poor horse's snout. She took off running as I turned away writhing and embarrassed at my stupidity. As I looked around to see who else saw what happened, I realized that no one had seen or heard the entire event—just Andie. About twenty minutes passed before my heartbeat returned to normal and my arm regained feeling.

My perception—even logical thinking—was trumped by reality. I cannot deny the fact that Andie was right, and I was wrong. (This could actually be a whole lesson in itself!) Sin is a reality in life. The consequential reality of sin is death (Romans 6:23). But there is a more important reality. "While we were still sinners, Christ died for us" (Romans 5:8). The need for a Savior is reality. Many perceived Jesus in the wrong way. They wanted an earthly king to overthrow the government. They wanted someone proud, powerful, and majestic. What they, and we, actually received was a baby, born humbly in a manger. When their perceptions and expectations did not become the reality they wanted, they crucified Jesus.

In your future endeavors, be sure to look deeper into the realities surrounding your perceptions. This is most essential in terms of communication. During my time in ministry, I have had a few parents complain about certain issues. Often, I have found that what they are complaining about is not the real, underlying issue that's really upsetting them. The only way to address their needs is to listen and work on the relationships. I had to keep in mind that while they, too, are sinners, Christ died for them. You can use the same thought process in your relationships with parents, significant others, co-workers, bosses, and even friends. The reality is God loves you. Now, go out and help others see that reality too.

Reflection

Perception and reality are in the eyes of the beholder. For a moment, consider yourself the beholder. Concepts and things with which you have experience may seem easy to you.

One example may be in the area of physical activity. You may be a skilled and courageous skateboarder. My perception is this: "If you can do it, it must be easy enough for me to do it too." The reality is me apologizing from a hospital bed for my disrespect—skateboarding being much more difficult than I had imagined.

Another example may be your nephew's difficulty with learning long division. If math is easy for you, you might not understand how it is so difficult for someone else—especially a relative. As you attempt to help your nephew, your voice becomes loud and shrill, as if life itself depended on nine divided by four. Your nephew stomps off, vowing to divide his time spent with you whenever you are together again. Your perception is that division is easy; his reality is that math challenges both cognition and relationships.

One final example is from the spiritual realm. How do you perceive your spirituality? Do you factor in Bible study, church attendance, deposits in your swear jar, number of Christian friends, and so forth?

How do you perceive your less religious or nonreligious friends? Do you see them only as other points of view? Or do they harbor beliefs that condemn them to hell? Is that reality too painful to consider? Reality can be much harsher than perception.

So which is more important, perception or reality? Silly question, right? Yet prevalent attitudes today seem to place much confidence in perceptions, allowing them to contain more authenticity and authority than they rightly deserve.

You will observe that some perceive God as a figment of imagination or the fantasy of fearful people. You may meet some who perceive God as an angry judge or a destructive deity. The reality of such perceptions threatens more than the eyes of the beholders. Sin perverts perceptions. And that *is* reality!

But there is another reality, independent of personal perceptions. Jesus Christ left His heavenly home to teach people the realities about God and themselves. He died not as the result of people angry about His teachings but because God sent Him to sacrifice His life for sinners, whether or not they perceive Him or their sin. And then Jesus died. Really died. No heartbeat, no other vitals. Dead. Dead for your sins and mine.

The reality did not end with His death. He rose from the dead. Came back to life. Poised to return for you and me, dead or alive, to take us to heaven.

Really? Really!

41

Stages of Life

Ephesians 5:25–27

As I spend time with more and more single young adults, I become more appreciative that God brought me Andie. I enjoyed my time being single, but marriage has been a new adventure every day that I share with my bride.

Marriage is the unique gift from God to demonstrate His love for the Church, but just because you are single does not mean you cannot fully understand God's love. Marriage is a relationship of sacrifices and commitments. God's relationship with His Bride, the Church, is the perfect example of that love—a relationship both marrieds and singles should strive to reflect.

Most of my friends were married before I was. I had difficulty watching them take that next step in adulthood while I was left in the dust. My married friends seemed to lose touch more than the single ones. That trend returned after I was married and when all my married friends started having kids. In my ministry, I have noticed the difficulty of singles relating to their peers who have children. The stages of life become too separated.

Singles do not have to worry about finding a sitter or realizing how long a trip to the grocery store takes. Couples forget the expense and difficulty of cooking for one. Singles don't have to worry about making two sets of holiday travel plans, whereas couples with kids might need to coordinate several different holiday plans. Those might not seem like big differences, but they do place you in different stages of life.

So what does an honoring relationship with God look like for these different stages of life?

Obviously, couples with kids are responsible to teach the faith about Jesus along with being nourished themselves. They need to work on their own relationships with God along with creating the best faith environment possible.

Singles have the challenge of finding a faith home that provides opportunities to serve and fosters growth in their relationships with God.

Couples have an accountability partner in this stage but also might be challenged if their partner does not have a strong faith life. All stages provide unique opportunities but also have their own tests.

No matter what stage you are in, make an attempt to fully understand and appreciate the benefits of that stage. As you face the challenges each stage presents, be sure to pass on your wisdom and experiences to others. Each stage creates different relationship opportunities.

As you encounter a new stage with new relationships, take a lesson from Scripture on how to love others:

> Husbands, love your wives, as Christ loved the Church and gave Himself up for her, that He might sanctify her, having cleansed her by the washing of water with the word, so that He might present the Church to Himself in splendor, without spot or wrinkle or any such thing, that she might be holy and without blemish. (Ephesians 5:25–27)

Remember, God loves you no matter what stage of life you are in. You are part of the Church and therefore a recipient of that amazing relationship He talks about in the Scriptures.

If you are struggling with being single, do not to rush into anything or try to force God's hand. Take time to pray and be present in your relationship with Him.

If you are a couple in need of support, or if you are a spouse in need of accountability that you do not have in your marriage, find a person of faith to help you.

If you have kids and feel a little drained or run down, rely on a faith community that offers training, support, and relief. The one constant in any stage of life is God. "Jesus Christ is the same yesterday and today and forever" (Hebrews 13:8), and He loves you.

Reflection

Aaron didn't mention one stage of life—the stage I am in now. Technically speaking, it is called *old*. But please avoid calling me that, even when I need suspenders to hold my pants up or take roll call of pills every morning. The new old was once *senior citizen*; the newer old is now *older adult*. I wonder what the next iteration will be. Eventually I will hit the *geezer* stage—if it does not hit me first.

Older adults are far from useless, unless they want to be. As they never age beyond being what the Bible (Revelation 19:1–10) calls the Bride of Christ (gender notwithstanding), they always have a calling, in sickness and health, here on earth and ever after in heaven.

The designation "in sickness and health" deserves some attention because both can come at any stage of life. Debilitating diseases and disabling injuries are not valid reasons for discontinuing the vocations God has called you to. They just change the way you serve.

One example may be the feeble Bride of Christ who witnesses his faith to the doctors and caretakers serving him. Or maybe it is an older adult, retired from employment but able to serve those confined to "homes" or who are homebound. Perhaps service to God and others happens through mentoring younger people through difficult stages of life. You never reach a stage of life useless for service, prayer, and praise.

The best stage of life is yet to come. Unlike stages matched to ages, the best stage can come at any time, even skipping the "normal" stages of life. The best stage is the final stage.

Humans cannot grasp the glory and pleasure of living in this stage. Try to imagine the best things of the previous stages of life and the absence of all the worst things of previous stages, and you will fall short of an adequate description of heaven. Go ahead and imagine anyway, but do not reserve such imagination only for the miserable times in other stages. Imagine them in the good times too, because whenever it seems that life could not be much better, it can. It will!

Until then, enjoy your present stage of life. Live life to the fullest (John 10:10), and serve God and His people with your best. Talk to God during each stage, and remember that no stage is sinless. No stage is without God's forgiveness and restoration either.

Now get out there. The stage awaits you.

42

Anxiety
Philippians 4:6–7

> Do not be anxious about anything, but in everything by prayer and supplication with thanksgiving let your requests be made known to God. And the peace of God, which surpasses all understanding, will guard your hearts and your minds in Christ Jesus. (Philippians 4:6–7)

Anxiety is plaguing Millennials, but they are not the only ones being targeted.

In a report from the American Psychological Association, the results of their *Stress in America* Survey point to Millennials being the most stressed generation ever. Stress causes anxiety, nervousness, irritability, anger, and feelings of being overwhelmed. But we read in Philippians to "not be anxious about anything." Is this expectation realistic for an overstressed Millennial or anyone?

I am on the older end of the Millennial Generation, and I do not consider myself a stressed person. I usually detach myself from the stressors of the day as long as I have some downtime. For about a year in my mid-twenties though, I was a victim of panic attacks. I could feel the stress building inside me. My vision would get cloudy, my legs restless, and my temperature would skyrocket. I wanted to do nothing but escape. These attacks typically happened right before I got up in front of a large crowd or when I had to meet someone for the first time. I was always nervous before times like these, but these new experiences with panic attacks were scary. I felt helpless. I felt weak.

I still cannot comprehend why such normal routines became so difficult for me or from where the attacks originated. I do not think they affected my performance or output, but I wanted them to stop. I came across Philippians 4:6–7 and tried the prayer route.

God's peace did not guard my heart and mind just because I prayed during a panic attack. Sure, He worked through His promises despite my own self getting in the way, but I continued to suffer the attacks. I prayed more and tried to dissect the origin of these thorns in my side. The answer was found not in my psychological well-being but in my relationship with God. I had not been in touch with Him. I forgot what His peace looks and feels like.

I returned to Scripture and to prayer journaling. With my recorded thoughts, I concluded that everything I was anxious about was actually harmless. The more I prayed, the more I felt the peace of God which surpasses all understanding. The key is that relationship with God. Prayer is a part of it, but the relationship extends beyond simply talking to God. It involves a lot of listening to His Word as well as recognizing His presence. The panic attacks became less regular, and eventually they ended altogether.

Your sinful nature wants you to know you are not good enough. Your sinful nature wants you to rely on yourself and to be overcome by anxiety and stress. The key word for me in Philippians is peace. A relationship with God provides a peace beyond understanding. This peace guards your heart and mind. You want others to experience this peace too. This peace is knowing there is nothing you need to do to be saved, because Jesus has already done it.

As you deal with stress and anxiety, I encourage you to strengthen your relationship with God. Pray, listen, and take time to see Him. If the stressors in your life are things you have power over, start with baby steps. Make little adjustments to your lifestyle, fostering the peace that only comes from God. If the stressors are not something you can control, then focus on your attitude or consider a lifestyle change.

As a victim in the most stressed generation, be a beacon of God's peace that makes other people question how and why. Then you can point them to Christ, the source of all hope, peace, and joy.

Reflection

Anxiety is common. But that does not make it good or something to tolerate. Anxieties may be laughable to others but rarely do sufferers see the humor. (Take heart. Hindsight sometimes offers comic relief.)

One of my former anxieties involved flying. No matter how hard I flapped, I just did not have the courage to actually leave the ground. Oh, sorry about that. I just wanted to see if you were paying attention.

Anyway, one of my former anxieties really did involve flying. As the aircraft would roll down the runway, I found myself praying, "Lord, please keep us safe." I prayed and prayed and prayed the same thing until wheels up. And though I flew often, I always prayed the same desperate words. Later, I thanked God, but the gratitude sounded suspiciously like I thought God might have missed my pleas had I not nagged. By the way, if my prayers ever became audible, the passengers sitting next to me seemed to exhibit a few anxieties themselves!

My runway prayers applied to additional situations: storms, household malfunctions, wild traffic, awaiting results of medical tests, and . . . the list is long. But does it not surprise you that a career church worker who has faithfully attended worship since infancy would have such anxieties?

It surprised me one day as I prayed Luther's Morning Prayer. One phrase goes like this: "For into Your hands I commend myself, my body and soul, and all things" (Small Catechism). Body, soul, all things—flying, reckless drivers, weather . . . all things? *Really*?

Anxiety, as I practiced it, betrayed my lack of trust in God. I knew what I wanted and so prayed in a way in which God would have a hard time ignoring. Oh, I usually remembered to say "If it is Your will," but I never took comfort in that phrase because I feared that my will and His will were mismatched.

That attitude and way of thinking demands repentance. The sin comes from not trusting God in all things, especially if all things include suffering, danger, and other unpleasantries. When Paul claimed, "And we know that for those who love God all things work together for good, for those who are called according to His purpose" (Romans 8:28), he meant *all* things—and he suffered many, many bad *all things*.

God does not promise you will avoid suffering. Sin infects the world with diseases, disasters, and devils. God does promise to bring you through them. You can trust Him with all things—you may even gain the advantage of fewer sleepless nights.

43

Being Your Own Boss

Ephesians 5:15–17

Are you your own boss? Now don't start fantasizing about six-hour work days and twelve weeks of vacation a year, or about making every Friday a tacky coffee mug day. Aside from the working world, are you your own boss?

This question actually has two parts. The first is about who manages what, or what manages who. Do you manage your time, or does your time manage you? You have dealt with this question most of your life, but you may have had help from your parents. Time is a valuable commodity and often a scarce resource. Have you found a comfortable and enjoyable groove yet?

Time management is mostly an issue of priorities. Back in chapter 16, I stressed the importance of scheduling rest into your routine. The motivation for that lesson came from spending time with a group of people whose time managed them. They had no time for rest, as their schedules were already too full. But does a full schedule mean you are living a full life?

The Bible talks about this issue in Ephesians: "Look carefully then how you walk, not as unwise but as wise, making the best use of the time, because the days are evil. Therefore do not be foolish, but understand what the will of the Lord is" (5:15–17).

How do you determine the "best use of the time?" Look a little deeper into Ephesians 5. It presents contrast between light and dark. Usually we think of disobedience as the darkness of something we do (sins of commission). Sometimes less apparent are the sins of omission, or the things we do not do that we should do. To make the best use of your time, you might have to leave your comfort zone for deeds of service that let your light shine. You might also have to check your own actions to make sure they align with the light and not the dark. Either way, you have to be your own boss and manager of your time. The first step to gaining control over your time is to schedule some rest.

The second part of the question about whether you are your own boss is about status. Do you lead through influence or by title? The best bosses never lord their titles over those under them. They do not resort to saying, "Do it because I said so and because I'm the boss!" The most effective leader has followers who are willingly invested in their leader's vision. In life, aside from work, there are many opportunities to be a leader.

You are not the boss of your friends or of your relationships, but you can still be a leader. The key to effectively leading also comes from Ephesians 5:1–2, which says, "Be imitators of God . . . and walk in love, as Christ loved us and gave Himself up for us." Effective leadership starts from a place of love. This second part also deals with time management. Are you building in time to love others?

It is nice to feel in control of your life. It is great to not be a victim of circumstance. But that does not always happen. In fact, rarely are we are in control of our own lives. Sin places a dark shroud over our minds, intentions, and actions. The light of Christ constantly battles the darkness.

Take solace in knowing that God is in control. He has already defeated the darkness of the tomb. It might be nice to feel in control, but it is even better to know that the One in control has your best interests at hand. He leads not by forcing obedience but by offering grace—a free gift, because we could not do it on our own. Continue to work on your priorities and on your relationship with the One who is in control.

Reflection

I think I had fooled myself into believing I was my own boss. Even during a period when I was deployed—working for two national organizations, having an office in my home, and under no day-to-day supervision—I was not my own boss. The refrigerator sometimes dominated, commanding me, "Come, get a cheese stick." Sometimes the dog insisted I play ball immediately. Then there was the "drowsy center" of my brain, which in accord with Aaron's advice, ordered me to "rest."

Being your own boss sounds like fun, but the joy associated with that often anchors itself in a disconnect with reality. The examples in the previous paragraph provide evidence. Being your own boss may not be good for you, either.

Productive bosses require self-confidence, which easily seeps into strong ego. Self-confidence may gorge on self-reliance, which practiced in extremes usually results in isolation, narrow mindedness, and faulty perceptions. This is true of those considering themselves their own bosses too.

Stifle aspirations to be your own boss. A better attitude is to recognize that almost every boss has a boss. Corporations operate on this principle, and it works well as long as all bosses are competent and know their places on the organizational chart.

Applying this concept to yourself, you work best when you recognize your competencies and confess that God is King of kings, Lord of lords, and Boss of bosses. The question now is how to assess your work. How and at what do you work best?

The answer begins with your training. What are your credentials? You attended mandatory grades and perhaps went on to trade school or to college to accumulate a series of letters—perhaps more than a few—behind your name. Your life experiences aside from formal education also prepared you. As good as these experiences may be, they are inadequate unless couched in a Christian, scriptural worldview.

Do not fret if you are weak in the latter. Connect with a congregation's Bible classes. Read on your own too, remembering to rely on guidance from a good study Bible. And stop thinking that the secular and the spiritual are two different realms of life. God is God of all things. He truly is Boss!

Being boss implies leadership. Good bosses are good leaders. (Good leaders are not always guaranteed boss-like titles, and boss-like titles do not always guarantee good leaders. Wow! Do you know that?) One element of being your own boss is how you lead others, once you have mastered—okay practiced—the art of being your own boss with God as your Boss.

You are in high demand as a leader. Loved ones and friends stand to benefit from your leadership. Again, the question is how best to accomplish the responsibility. Jesus (Kings of kings, Lord of lords, Boss of bosses) said:

> You know that those who are considered rulers of the Gentiles lord it over them, and their great ones exercise authority over them. But it shall not be so among you. But whoever would be great among you must be your servant, and whoever would be first among you must be slave of all. For even the Son of Man came not to be served but to serve, and to give His life as a ransom for many. (Mark 10:42–45)

If you want to be your own boss, be the best: Serve others with the blessings God has given you. Assume leadership. Tell others what Jesus did for you. Live in harmony with what you tell others—and that includes asking and receiving forgiveness for your failures. And take a day off once in a while. Spend it in conversation with Jesus. You will find it an enjoyable way to rest.

44

Trusting the Pilot

Psalm 9:10

A long day was just about over. Typically, my energy level started to diminish after the Wednesdays of band-tour weeks, but it was only Tuesday. The long drives, set-ups and take-downs, and the sometimes odd—or, uh, interesting—people we stayed with had us "working" eighteen-hour days. But the next day was a free day at the beach—one more night and then we could relax. But our host family seemed like talkers.

"The night just got longer," I remember muttering to Nathan, my tour partner.

Nathan just smiled, and we loaded the car. The host family had driven two cars, and the wife had already left, so we hopped into the husband's pick-up truck and asked the usual questions: "How long have you lived here? Did you enjoy the concert? Do you have any kids? What do you do? His response to our last question piqued our interest. He was a pilot, and he lived next to an airport. He chuckled as he gave his response, and when we arrived at his house, we found out why. He did not live *next* to an airport; he practically lived *at* the airport. The view from his front door was a tall, barbed wire fence and the blinking lights of the runway.

After we unloaded our luggage, he told us to hop back in the truck.

He wanted to show us the plane he owned. The night was starting to look better and better. The drive around the block revealed another surprise. Not only was he a pilot, but he was also a flight instructor! His two-seater Bellanca was a beautiful, red machine. I jumped in the cockpit first, while Nathan called his girlfriend to share the exciting news.

The flight instructor explained everything as if he were about to train a new pilot. I listened closely and found out about the throttle, flaps, and rudder. We taxied out to the runway and received clearance from the tower to do some touch-and-go circuits. He explained the surroundings on our first circle of the airport. As we lined up for an approach, he explained the purpose of the different lights along the runway.

The tower had already gone dark for the night, so we were flying by a sophisticated satellite tracking system. That scared me a little, but this man whom I had met just a few hours ago seemed knowledgeable. After our first touch-and-go, he told me to take the second set of controls and feel how he used them. Our ascent took us up and around, and we ran a second touch-and-go. As soon as the wheels left the runway, he told me the plane was mine.

WHAT?

In my excited panic, I pulled up on the controls and let the throttle out as we gained altitude. I was surprised at how easy it was to fly a plane. Our circle around the airport took us in view of a jumbo jet with the UPS logo on the tail. The pilot told me to relax and stretch out the circle a little, as he wanted me to land behind the jumbo jet. Having no knowledge of flying or landing (other than what I had just learned), I obeyed completely.

The instructor warned me that jumbo jets disturb the air, so we might feel turbulence. I reminded him I had never flown and asked again, "Are you sure you want me to land?"

"Don't worry, just listen to my voice."

Very carefully, the landing gear kissed the pavement, and we were on the ground.

Don't worry, just listen to my voice.

When this command comes from God, why are we so quick to argue or disobey? My life was in my hands in the cockpit of that plane. I could listen to the instructor, or I could disobey. Disobedience would mean chaos or even death. Compliance and submission in the capable hands of a trustworthy pilot meant that I would be okay.

The psalm at the beginning of this lesson reminds us that God does not forsake the ones He loves. He is faithful. The pilot knew everything about flying his plane. God knows everything about life. He even wrote a book, the Bible. In this instruction manual, He lays down rules and laws. He shows us those who broke those laws and became miserable. He also provides examples of those who are faithful and obedient.

But the Bible is not simply a "to-do" or "not-to-do" book. The Bible is a narrative about God's love. We cannot follow His Law perfectly, and we get caught in turbulence, but in those times He tells us, "Don't worry, just listen to my voice." His grace and forgiveness allow us to keep flying. We would be dead in our sin if not for the gift of His Son. Our hope would be gone if not for the restoring work of the Holy Spirit.

He loves you and is a more than capable pilot to lead you through life.

Reflection

I did not know Aaron would have the opportunity to fly on his band tour. The most risky thing I suspected was a drum solo—when the score did not call for one. Had he called to ask permission, I would have said, "No!" plus a few other things.

I learned several lessons here. The first was that sometimes it is good not to know what is happening. I would have paced, questioned my son's intelligence, and prayed the kinds of untrusting prayers that I mentioned in a previous chapter. As for the "all things" commended to God in Luther's Morning Prayer, flying would not have been one of them. As I said, sometimes it is good to be unaware. That attitude has spiritual merit too.

Believers are protectively unaware of what the devil is doing out of sight in all-out efforts to have them crash and burn in hell. You and I do not see the spiritual battles to claim our souls. Satan knows Jesus' complete victory on the cross will bring about his utter defeat (Romans 8:38–39). Mortal wounds make him a fierce fighter. The battle is best left beyond our perception.

I also realize that God does not need my help. He is the Pilot for all believers on their journeys to Judgment Day. That includes people I love dearly and those who have been entrusted to my care. He invites my prayers, but He does not need them. Neither worry nor fear nor skepticism help. The Pilot is trustworthy.

The most important lesson for me was really just a review. I am not always in charge. Christians desire happy endings to their story. They don't want turbulence to shake their lives. They trust and follow the Pilot even when life is peaceful and calm.

But so much depends on how you define "happy ending." Christians suffer and die—even the "best" of them. Some of them die horribly. But suffering and death do not affect our salvation, and at the end of the story we are victorious. For the Pilot says this:

> For I am sure that neither death nor life, nor angels nor rulers, nor things present nor things to come, nor powers, nor height nor depth, nor anything else in all creation, will be able to separate us from the love of God in Christ Jesus our Lord." (Romans 8:38–39)

45

Signature Sauce

Matthew 5:13–16

What is your signature sauce? I'm not talking about a mango cilantro chutney or plain old barbeque sauce but your "flavor." Perhaps a better way of asking this question is, "What will you be remembered for after you die?" Let's look at the word *flavor* a little more.

When I cook I season food accordingly—well, most times. Scent plays an important role in mixing spices that essentially affect the final flavor of the food. Under-seasoned or over-seasoned food tastes unpleasant or leaves a negative impact on your eating experience. Improperly cooked food can also cause stomach problems or a lot of crunchy, strenuous chewing. Cooking is an art, and it takes a careful hand to create the perfect dish. Think about all those cookbooks on bookstore shelves. Contained in those books are thousands of precisely measured instructions. There are few areas in life for which we have cookbooks.

In cooking, sauces cover the need to precisely pull the pork roast out of the oven when it hits 165 degrees or to remove the steak with a juicy pink center from the grill. Sauces allow more freedom to deviate from recipes or add more flavors. Many sauces flavor life too.

Think of life recipes. If you go to school, choose the right friends, follow the rules, and work hard, you will succeed. But if you party too much, don't study enough, and goof around all the time, the result is like an unseasoned dish with an unpleasant aftertaste. At least that is what the recipe says, right?

Life recipes are changing. No longer does a college degree guarantee a good job upon graduation. Even a master's degree doesn't ensure a job. Hard work no longer sets you above others. Who has time for friendships when there are so many résumés to write and research projects to be done? Rules are subjective and have different meanings to each person. Some life recipes seem outdated.

So why not improve the situation by developing your own signature sauce?

Adam and Eve had a recipe for happiness. All they had to do was *not* eat from a certain tree. Moses had a recipe that he kept changing. Eventually, his adjustments prevented him from entering the Promised Land. Jonah had a recipe. All he had to do was go to an evil city and tell the inhabitants about God's wrath if they did not change their ways—perhaps this recipe was a little more complicated. His deviation landed him in the belly of a fish.

God could have allowed His creation to stumble and fall apart. Instead, He added His signature sauce—a sauce filled with love and grace—a sauce that makes life possible and leaves an aftertaste of hope. He served His prized sauce in a recipe He gave to Mary and Joseph. Their recipe was hard to follow at first, but the result was an outstanding delicacy. They obeyed God and trusted His recipe. They raised the Savior of the world.

How can you develop your signature sauce? It will never be as good as God's, but it can help to distinguish you. How will you season your sauce? Look at Matthew 5:13–16 for a start, specifically verse 16: "In the same way, let your light shine before others, so that they may see your good works and give glory to your Father who is in heaven."

Throw in a few cups of being salt and light in the world. Add a heaping tablespoon of trust and a healthy dose of putting others before yourself. Drop in tons of forgiveness and love. Throw in a pinch of Sabbath rest, and layer it every day with God's Word.

Reflection

Sauces require something on which to put them—and not just anything, either. For example, a butter/oil/garlic/white pepper sauce (Bordelaise) would not taste good on strawberry ice cream. Chocolate sauce over Brussels sprouts might make the sprouts slide down easier to your stomach, but it is a terrible thing to do to chocolate. Use those same sauces but switch the foods and you have winners. Sauces used properly are gifts of good eating.

Have you considered that God has "sauced" you? The Bible reminds us:

> Having gifts that differ according to the grace given to us, let us use them: if prophecy, in proportion to our faith; if service, in our serving; the one who teaches, in his teaching; the one who exhorts, in his exhortation; the one who contributes, in generosity; the one who leads, with zeal; the one who does acts of mercy, with cheerfulness. (Romans 12:6–8)

God blessed you with some of those gifts. They are the sauces with which He flavors you, His creation. Oh, and like the best of sauces, your blessings need not be dramatic. They blend into your life and become part of your total "flavor." I will share with you some examples.

Aaron enjoys cooking and does it well. He uses this "sauce" to literally serve his wife, his congregation, and even a hungry community.

You might enjoy helping others who cannot get their computer, remote, or game to work right. You, then, are sauced not only with technological knowledge but also with the gift of teaching—in service to another.

Are you a good exhorter? When is the last time you went about exhorting? If you encourage someone on a task or cheer someone on, you have the snappy exhortation sauce. Use it to flavor a co-worker's life or even your pastor's life. Be liberal in encouraging children who need a lift of spirits or a spurt of persistence on their homework. You do not need to be rich to be laced with contributor sauce. So many needs beg your attention, so choose wisely what or whom you support. Check into the backgrounds of organizations seeking your generosity.

As Aaron mentioned, sauces can cover mistakes and imperfections. These conditions find God liberally ladling on forgiveness and restoration. Scripture addresses this in 1 Peter 4:8, which says, “Keep loving one another earnestly, since love covers a multitude of sins.”

While that verse is Peter’s exhortation to us, it also is Jesus’ practice toward us. Love and forgiveness are the sauces that allow us to serve though imperfectly, to exhort though weakly, and to help though flawed.

Enjoy your sauces. Share them with others.

46

SELFISHNESS

Romans 15:1–2

A popular business model illustrates a successful entrepreneur as someone who uses the people below him as steps to climb to the top. I took a small-business class that helped me develop a feasibility study for a business I was interested in starting. The class was filled with many small-business owners looking to better their businesses, along with others interested in starting businesses. We also had many successful business owners share words of wisdom. One message was consistent, and it bothered me: you have to step on others in order to reach the top.

Whereas this might be a popular business method, it is not biblical. Romans 15:1–2 says, "We who are strong have an obligation to bear with the failings of the weak, and not to please ourselves. Let each of us please his neighbor for his good, to build him up."

A second reference is what Jesus calls the Great Commandment: love God and love one another (Matthew 22:37–40). How can you love others while stepping on them? Do not prey on the weaknesses of others; rather, find a way to build them up and offer support.

Selfishness is a big issue outside of the business world too. When you are single, you tend do things that benefit only you. Your focus tends to be on your own betterment rather than on the advancement of others. Think about it. This is the time in your life where you advance your career and put yourself into a state of financial progress. Can there be a balance?

Yes, this is where service can be helpful. Serving with humility opens your eyes to the plight of the world and inspires an appreciation for your position in life. Even if you are not single, your focus can often be selfish and create the business-ladder effect. Do your actions need a little adjustment? What other ways can you serve your neighbor rather than self?

Rather than stepping on people to get ahead, is there a way to help someone else up the ladder? Perhaps you are already on a higher rung. Can you lean down and help someone else up? Being solo on a ladder is never a good idea. It helps to have someone on the ground holding the ladder, playing the support role. Can you play a supporting role in someone else's life?

The balance of success and support can be difficult—especially at this point in your life. Consider a basketball team. There are supporting roles and starring roles. Each relies heavily on the other if the team is to be successful. Both are important and necessary. Look at John the Baptist (Matthew 3:1–17). He was number one in success as droves of people sought him out to be baptized, but when Jesus came, John quickly changed from the star to the supporting role.

What role has God called you to fulfill? This role might change too. Will you be ready? As a Christian, you are called to build up the weak and love your neighbor. Your success is important but not at the expense of others. Jesus gave His life, taking upon Himself the shortcomings of others. He climbed that cross for us and reached down out of love to lift us up from the world of sin. Quite the opposite of stepping on us, huh?

Reflection

You started at rock bottom.

Psalm 51:5 says, "Behold, I was brought forth in iniquity, and in sin did my mother conceive me." Oh, you probably were cute and cuddly, but you also were sinful. You inherited sin that goes all the way back to Adam and Eve.

Sin drives one to selfishness. It happens from the time you were young to now. Just observe two young children and one popular toy. Or consider the preflight flurry of passengers jockeying for boarding spots that give them access to overhead bins. Worse, of course, is Aaron's example of stepping on others for self-promotion.

All this, however, leaves an important question. How do you get ahead in the world if you are not selfish?

Jesus has the answer. He said, "If anyone would be first, he must be last of all and servant of all" (Mark 9:35). Considering that Jesus *is* on the top rung of any ladder, His authority and divine wisdom back His Word on this. Worldly philosophy does not support it, and observation of some of the most successful people in the world would not testify to its truth, because selfishness backed by power and skill often yields earthly success.

Or does it?

Jesus was talking to His disciples in the quote from Mark. They had selfishness issues too. Jesus even caught a few of them debating their rank among the other disciples. How would they become the star player on/of Jesus' team? By serving others! Do you suppose that made sense to them? Would it make sense to your friends and colleagues? Your family?

Serving others sounds like "church behavior." You would serve others by working tables at the Men's Club Ham Hock Dinner or staffing the dunk tank at the church picnic. And maybe you could serve in the community by volunteering for street-corner collections for the firefighters' benefit fund or other worthy local causes.

Serving others is not just church behavior. Service is the mark of Christians living in gratitude to God Himself, who lifted them up from the bottom.

A servant attitude does not automatically doom your aspirations for career advancement. Servant hearts are noticed, as you cheerfully go about helping others. People learn to trust you for your kindness and integrity. (Okay, some will also learn to step on you. Suck it up. Persist anyway. That is what the disciples did.) Favorable impressions from those who have served may open doors to advancement, but something more important happens.

People may wonder why you are the way you are. They may even be bold to ask how you got "that way." And here is your big chance!

Tell them how you started at the bottom. (Many people believe they began life innocent and pure.) Tell them what Jesus did for you, how His life, death, and resurrection made you what you are, despite your ongoing battle with sinfulness—which He regularly forgives. Tell them how Jesus added you to His centuries-old team of servants and wants everyone to be on His team.

Will everyone glow after hearing your report? What do you think? The realities of servanthood can be difficult or even harsh. Ask the Holy Spirit to strengthen and comfort you. And remember that the Savior—the almighty God Himself—served even to the point of dying, to save the lives of sinners.

47

Love, Not Hate, Except . . .

1 John 4:19–21

Christians do not often hold the most popular opinion when it comes to politics or sensitive subjects. Oftentimes, what the Bible says contradicts what is culturally or even legally acceptable. Does that mean the Bible is outdated or impractical?

No.

The Bible is truth and transcends time. It is a book of laws, but, more important, it highlights God's grace and love to humanity in desperate need of saving. When it comes to sensitive subjects and discussions with people who might not be familiar with the Bible, take a lesson from the apostle John:

> We love because He first loved us. If anyone says, "I love God," and hates his brother, he is a liar; for he who does not love his brother whom he has seen cannot love God whom he has not seen. And this commandment we have from Him: whoever loves God must also love his brother. (1 John 4:19–21)

John says we cannot harbor hate. Is certain behavior wrong or sinful? Yes. We see those behaviors outlined in the Bible. Trying to justify certain behaviors or subjectively defining the Law can get you in trouble. The devil trapped Eve that way. The downward spiral created from justifying wrong behaviors or attitudes can quickly get out of control.

Beyond trying to tweak the Law or justifying behavior is straight up hate and judgment. When you think of yourself as better than someone else, you judge them and put them in a state that is lower than you. For example, Christians and non-Christians alike often judge presidents—easy targets because of their high-profile position. Rather than throw up a meme on Facebook about your disapproval, why not pray for the president? Pleasing even a roomful of people is difficult, let alone an entire nation! Our leaders need our prayers and godly people to surround them, regardless of our personal feelings about them.

All sins are equal in the eyes of the Lord and worthy of eternal damnation. James 2:10 says, "For whoever keeps the whole law but fails in one point has become accountable for all of it."

Any failure, as slight as it might be, is cause for punishment. And the punishment for being sinful is death. Some sins have earthly consequences that are worse than others, but whether it is a little white lie or a mass murder, the eternal consequence is hell.

Praise God for sending His Son! "If we confess our sins, He is faithful and just to forgive us our sins and to cleanse us from all unrighteousness" (1 John 1:9). Our eternal punishment is taken away! There is no room for judgment and hate to exist in the believer's heart. God's love takes up a lot of room.

Two things to take away from this lesson:

1. God's Word is alive and still applicable.
2. Pray rather than judge.

Be an example of Christ when discussing issues about which you may have a difference of opinion. Reflect on your opinions and see if they align with what God says in Scripture.

Remember that "all have sinned and fall short of the glory of God" (Romans 3:23) and that you are no better than anyone else. Paul provides a proper summary in 2 Corinthians 5:14–15:

> For the love of Christ controls us, because we have concluded this: that one has died for all, therefore all have died; and He died for all, that those who live might no longer live for themselves but for Him who for their sake died and was raised.

As we live out our faith, we serve as examples of Christ's work in our lives.

Reflection

I must caution Aaron on a transgressional, personal technicality. With all he said about hate and love, he will need to cool his White Sox-fueled hate of the Cubs.

Aaron never actually lived on the south side of Chicago as I did, so I fear that he learned his hate from me, because native South Siders often have Cub-hate inscribed somewhere on their stem cells. Passed along from generation to generation, the contempt grows with each losing Cubs' season and even more with every winning Cubs season!

The Bible is clear about what to do with people you hate. Love them (Matthew 5:43–47). Love them even if they do not want your love. Love them even if they hate you. And, yes, love them even if they are the Cubs. But how do you change hate into love?

Perhaps the easiest way is to pray for them. After a while, you will find it difficult to hate those for whom you pray. But just how far do you extend these prayers? Again, Jesus provides an answer—from the cross where He asked the Father to forgive those responsible for His death (Luke 23:34).

Uh-oh. Did you catch that last sentence—"those responsible for His death"? That includes you and me. The sins of all people caused Christ's death.

While we are considering hate, here is an important question: is hate ever appropriate?

I mean, is hating asparagus or sauerkraut wrong? Probably. Consider that God was angry when the children of Israel whined about having to eat manna day in and day out. Mind you, manna was God's miracle to keep them alive. God did not teach them to enjoy manna; instead, He sent them meat, which they gobbled down with disastrous effect (Numbers 11).

Life with God is much more serious than asparagus or other culinary unpleasantries. Hate often plays a righteous role, so when is hate good?

Scripture clearly speaks to that question, especially in Amos 5:15, which says, "Hate evil, and love good."

Forgive this personal question, but please do answer it in your mind. Do certain sins beset you? Do you find that you commit the same sin over and over? Do you repeatedly omit doing good in specific situations?

The common answer is yes from all people—unless they altogether deny their sinfulness. So you are in good company . . . maybe that should be *bad* company. Your company includes such notables as King David and the apostle Paul—even after his conversion. Human nature interferes with even the noblest attempts at perfect, godly living. What to do?

Hate!

Hate sin. Sometimes that is all you can do. Guilt tells you when to do it. Repentance provides the process for it. God through Jesus Christ provides forgiveness, and the Holy Spirit feeds your fire to hate and fight it.

48

Waiting
John 8:1–11

Growing up, I always wanted to get a good job, get married, have kids, own a house, own a boat, and live the American dream (in that order). I can cross three of those off my list. (And my homeowner experience is *not* what I envision when I think of the American dream!) I always thought by the time I turned thirty all these items would be crossed off my list. Life takes some interesting twists and turns.

According to the Pew Research Center, Millennials are waiting longer to get married. Only 26 percent of people ages eighteen to thirty-two are married. I find it interesting that a majority of this age group wants to be married but lacks a solid economic foundation, which they deem necessary to get married.

Marriage is a lifelong commitment, a big decision, and a significant change to your life. No longer are you one, but two. Marriage should not be entered into lightly or in haste. However, since people are waiting longer and longer to get married, other challenges arise. Many of those not seeking lifelong partners engage in pre-marital sex to satisfy their urges. Others are caught up in pornography or have children out of wedlock. Many who seek spouses take intimacy to the physical level too quickly and never fully experience God's plan for their unions.

Sex has an influence on everything from television, music, and the magazine rack to clothing choices, books, and youth group discussions. It is not a new topic either. The Bible contains many stories about this misused blessing from God. Lot's daughters slept with him after getting him drunk (Genesis 19:30–38); Potiphar's wife unsuccessfully attempted to seduce Joseph (Genesis 39); and good King David took Bathsheba, another man's wife, and had her husband killed (2 Samuel 11). The New Testament talks about Jesus hanging out with prostitutes and adulterers, even a woman caught in the act (John 8:1–11). The misuse of sex has been around for quite a long time.

God created us with the ability and desire for sex but within certain parameters. Hebrews 13:4 explains those standards most clearly: "Let marriage be held in honor among all, and let the marriage bed be undefiled."

Sex is a glorious gift from God but can cause hardships when misused. Culture has desensitized us to sex crimes, one-night stands, and affairs. People are sold into sexual slavery or stand on street corners to make ends meet. Lives are changed because of STDs and unplanned pregnancies.

With roughly 75 percent of the Millennial population unmarried, sex can be a serious temptation. Have you waited, or have you given in to your urges? God loves you—even if you haven't waited. His blood washes you clean, and you are reconciled to Him. In the account of the woman caught in adultery (John 8:1–11), Jesus does not condone her behavior, but He also does not condemn her. You are not worthless, dirty, or a failure in Jesus' eyes. You are His beloved child—a child that shares in His sacrifice and promise. Pray for the strength to resist sexual temptation, but do not lose hope when you fail. His perfection trumps the need for your perfection. Trust His promises and trust His love.

Reflection

Waiting, waiting, waiting, waiting, waiting, waiting, waiting, waiting, waiting, and waiting more. You experience it in all of life, and, now, even in a sentence about waiting. Waiting for marital fulfillment might occupy your mind right now, but waiting for other things becomes more prevalent as you age.

Waiting is bad enough when the bus is off schedule or the checkout clerk calls for a price check. Waiting causes anxiety when you do it at the dentist's office or in a courtroom. And waiting is more annoying than it should be at that great restaurant that has good food and sloth-like wait staff. Perhaps the most challenging wait is that which surrounds relationships.

Do you have a best friend, or are you still ardently waiting for one? And once you have a dog, what— Oh, sorry, not that kind of best friend? Best friends (a.k.a. BFFs in younger circles) are important and worth the wait to be selective. After all, you will trust your best friend with all manner of personal information. And he or she will want the same treatment.

The best friend category includes spouses too. God blessed Aaron in his immediate post-university life. He and Andie connected quickly; their wait was relatively short. My wait for Renee spread over several lonely years. God blessed the waiting in both cases. Waiting for the deepest intimacies of marriage made our relationships stronger.

The Bible reports some record relationship waits. The shortest wait might belong to Adam, Eve, and God. No sooner had Adam and Eve sinned their way out of their first home than God promised a Savior to take away their sins (Genesis 3).

Record long waits are common in Scripture too. Consider the children of Israel who waited four hundred years for freedom from slavery. Then they spent an additional forty years wandering the wilderness before they entered their Promised Land.

Awaiting fulfillment of God's aforementioned promise in Genesis 3 set some records too. Some scholars set that wait at about four thousand years—enough time to lose faith in a promise but also enough time to ponder a lot of lessons.

One of those lessons involves God's relationship with His children: you, me, and millions of others—past, present, and future.

You may not think of this at your present age, but the longer you live, the more likely you are to ask, "What is God waiting for?" (If you are good at English, you would ask, "For what is God waiting?) In other words, why is God waiting to initiate Judgment Day?

Jesus promised to return. That was more than two thousand years ago. You might be tempted to think His promise was empty. You have, however, the comfort of knowing about the Savior's first promise, so just wait and wait and wait and wait and . . . Your waiting may end in the next minute. Or . . .

Again, you may ask, "What is God waiting for?" He is waiting for the "right time." Until the "right time," we wait, trusting that when God says the time is right, we will see Jesus and join Him in heaven. Be assured that He will find a way around waiting in long lines to get in! Once in, you will never wait for anything again.

Unless you wait for heaven to end. That wait will set a new, unbreakable record.

49

Transformer or Conformer?

Romans 12:2

All of our life lessons share a common undertone: "Do not be conformed to this world, but be transformed by the renewal of your mind, that by testing you may discern what is the will of God, what is good and acceptable and perfect" (Romans 12:2). Two words stick out in this verse: *conform* and *transform*.

My brother-in-law loves Transformers toys. His collection would make serious toy collectors jealous. Transformers change from something ordinary into something extraordinary. The disguises they use are common or practical, but in their transformed state, they become robots able to save the human race.

Butterflies are also transformed creatures. They start as caterpillars just inching around. After their transformation, they are beautiful creatures of flight able to experience much more than the branch of a tree. Is this what Paul is talking about in Romans?

Paul himself was transformed. On the road to Damascus, he was transformed by God's power (Acts 9). His life went from one of persecuting those who followed Christ to leading others to Christ. As his attitude and outlook changed, so did his life. He even explains how to be transformed by telling us to not be conformed to this world, but rather to follow God's will.

This is somewhat depressing information.

Paul implies that the world will always be against us. Jesus even says, "You will be hated by all for My name's sake" (Matthew 10:22). A big challenge lies in the life of a Christian. Following God is not easy. Paul advises us, "Be transformed by the renewal of your mind" (Romans 12:2).

Renewal is usually a good thing, but it usually costs something. Renewing a subscription costs money. Taking a weekend vacation for rest and renewal costs time. Renewing an old, broken relationship costs humility. What does a renewing of your mind cost?

The word *renew* implies that something is worn out, weak, or in need of an extension. Does that describe your current way of thinking?

Staying fresh with God's way of thinking requires daily time in His Word, repentance, and constantly challenging your "old self." Your old self always wants to conform to this world. Your old self sabotages your attitudes, pushing you to violate God's Word, much like Satan's attack on "old Adam" and "old Eve." They conformed to the world even before that standard was set. They were transformed from a God-like image of perfection to a dying breed of pathetic sinners. To know perfection and watch it slip away must have been beyond frustrating. They went from fresh to rotten with one simple act.

Just as with Adam and Eve, God did not leave you to rot in your old self. Through the waters of Baptism, the Holy Spirit renews you and transforms you into a new self. This suggests another common undertone throughout these lessons (actually, it's more an overtone): grace.

God frees us from the eternal consequences of sin with His love and sacrifice. He gives us a new life and yet another chance. Even with a renewed mind, we cannot obey the Law perfectly and end up conforming to our own will, but that is why Jesus came. Born humbly in a manger, God became man and lived with us. He gave His life as payment for our sins, and we belong to Him.

Stay fresh and renewed no matter what the cost, because the payout will be eternity with Him. Your transformation will not be complete until the day when you meet the Savior face to face, but fight conforming to this world so that you do not slip away. As you grow in your faith and experience more of what life has to offer, please do not walk away from Him. He loves you and will never leave you. May that message have transformational power for your mind and actions!

REFLECTION

I hate, whoops, I mean I dislike when Aaron writes all the good stuff on a topic and leaves me with a mental block. But consider the following: Once upon a time, transformers referred mostly to the black box that controlled model trains. They transformed incoming electricity to voltage tame enough not to transform trains to molten messes.

Transformers also loomed in larger forms atop utility poles, which, in my neighborhood, served as a convenient enabler of squirrel suicides in most dramatic fashion. Their more benign—but still potentially threatening—use tamed wild voltage into something useful. Being too old to relate to the Transformers of Aaron's and my son-in-law's ages, I think electrical transformers offer some powerful spiritual meditation.

Be transformed indeed! God has wired you for transforming Scripture's power into acts of faith. When the Holy Spirit delivered water-generated faith into your soul, it was not for the sole purpose of having somewhere to store it. As you have read before, "For we are His workmanship, created in Christ Jesus for good works, which God prepared beforehand, that we should walk in them" (Ephesians 2:10).

God's Word, from cover to cover, reports the history of God's love for His creation. History honestly records dark days as well as great moments in faith—most of which involve God's faithfulness to His children rather than vice versa. That history continues today, just not in biblical format.

Through Baptism, the Holy Spirit not only provides faith in knowing that Jesus is your Savior but also zaps you with power to share that faith.

Your transformation need not be dramatic like Paul's change from his Saul days (Acts 9) or like Moses' transformation from shy, inarticulate, and timid to leader of the children of Israel's exodus from slavery (Exodus 3). (Note: If a burning bush talks to you, call the fire department. Today, God works through His Word rather than flaming flora.)

Your transformation brings on a mind awash with a biblical worldview. You know that God is God of everything, not just God of what happens in worship or Bible class. Your actions are influenced by your ever-increasing knowledge of Scripture, from which you have a string of lessons about the actions of believers, both weak and strong, and God's relationship with both.

And so we return to the beginning. Romans 12:2 says, "Do not be conformed to this world, but be transformed by the renewal of your mind, that by testing you may discern what is the will of God, what is good and acceptable and perfect."

Ephesians 2:10, as well as other passages—such as Romans 12:2, may be repeated in this book, but it's not for a lack of verses—there are more than thirty-one thousand of them. Bible passages are meant to be used and reused; they are so rich in what God wants us to know that they can spark new meanings every time you reread one. They keep on transforming!

50

HELP WITH ANXIETY

Hebrews 10:23–25

The Central Illinois District DCEs are the reason I am still in ministry. Fresh out of college, I experienced some major hardships in my first job that pushed me to the brink of quitting. I tried interviewing for other positions, but the interviews were not producing job offers. My situation was not improving, and the work environment was toxic. I spent more time in meetings reporting on my workday and justifying my actions than I did in ministry with people. I never knew my life would be under such scrutiny . . . especially in a church!

I had my resignation letter written and in hand many times. Instead of giving up, I continued to fight, but the fight was taking its toll. Slowly, the fight wore me down. Praise God I was not alone.

Two DCEs in the area had been through similar struggles. They offered listening ears and shared their past trials until their once-safe environment broke down as well. Both were asked to resign. Was this ministry? Why is anyone still in ministry if it causes so much anxiety and stress? How can a church be such a harsh environment? Shouldn't a church be a safe place?

Anxiety controls your mind. Every little detail becomes a major problem. The result is stress and feeling overwhelmed. Hope diminishes and panic ensues. Rather than fight, you prefer flight. And sometimes running from the problem is the only solution. Look at David in 1 Samuel 19–23. Saul is king. He's in charge. He does not trust David and makes multiple attempts to kill him. There is no future for David while Saul is in charge. He runs and flees but only for a time. Throughout the Psalms, you can witness David's faith in God and God's fulfillment of His promise to keep David safe. David also had a following and support system of people.

I found solace in knowing I was not alone in my trials, but I was still ready to quit. I looked to God to rescue me and get me out of my situation. His time was not my time, and I still had lessons to learn. I learned how to rely on others and network with them in order to accomplish His work. Besides my two colleagues in town, I had a group of ten or twelve other church workers all ready to hear me out and build me up.

The various levels of experience really made that group a strong support network. Some had been in the field as long as I had, others for ten years, and still others for more than twenty years. I looked to these people for the solution to longevity in ministry. Obviously, they had found a way to work through the stressful and unhealthy times to continue being a part of the kingdom of God. But it was not the advice they gave that made this group so helpful. It was the encouragement they offered, as well as the challenges they pushed me to conquer.

Family and friends were also supportive. I never feared, even if I lost (or quit) my job, because I could always fall back on their support. My future wife and her family also helped me through this time, and many people in the congregation still encouraged me and supported my work.

Support from family and friends is often colored with love. This kind of support is extremely helpful but often defends more than spurs. My DCE group spurred me on. Yet sometimes spurs hurt. When a cowboy digs his spurs into a horse, the horse responds. As the relationship becomes more trusting and predictable, less pressure is needed from the spur. My group pushed hard at first but never let me wander too far off the path.

> Let us hold fast the confession of our hope without wavering, for He who promised is faithful. And let us consider how to stir up one another to love and good works, not neglecting to meet together, as is the habit of some, but encouraging one another, and all the more as you see the Day drawing near. (Hebrews 10:23–25)

God provides other Christians to help you through the hard times. A Christian support network has been extremely valuable to me.

Do you have a Christian support network—a group of people familiar with God's plan? How can you be an encouraging and spurring part of this group in return? Do you completely trust that God is faithful? And beyond your own needs, how could someone benefit from your support?

I failed at having an unwavering hope. But even in my stubbornness and lack of faith, my story ends (or continues on?) with accepting a call to a congregation where I have healed. In this emotionally healthy environment, I am encouraged to continue in ministry as well as pay it forward. As my current DCE group meets, I offer my support, encouragement, spurring, and love. Keep your eyes open for those opportunities and live with a hope that is unwavering. Rely on God and live interdependently with that vast network of other Christians.

Reflection

I thank God for Aaron's colleagues, friends, and family. I pray that you have support through trials, as I know you will have them. God does not promise an easy life for any believer, not even church workers. Not even highly successful people in other vocations.

What will you do with your anxieties? The lesson seems clear. Do not deal with them alone. Doing so will magnify them, perhaps even drive you into despair or depression—two places you do not want to be, especially alone.

Friends and family can help. The professional staff at your church may be helpful too, if for nothing else than to connect you with people more equipped to help. Are you short on friends, distant from family, or not associated with a Christian congregation? Not to pontificate or nag, but work toward such relationships in good times rather than in the bad times.

The key word being *work*. Relationships take work as you meet people and spend time with them. Take time to seek out Christian friends at work and socialize with them. Yes, Christians can have fun! Keep in touch with family through visits, phone calls, or text messages. Find a group or activity in your church that offers interaction and service projects, which need not be limited to your age group. Intergenerational friends offer wisdom and experience to help you grow.

One more thing, do all of the above with the intent of contributing to the happiness and health of the people already in those groups. They need you, and the more time you spend thinking of them, the less time you will have to worry about yourself.

51

The Truth in Reality

2 Samuel 22:31

What is real and what is not? In a society of photo-shopped images, edited videos, and skewed news reports, what is real? Another way to ask this is, "What is truth?"

As election years come and go, the media bombards the public with mudslinging and ads that expose flaws in various candidates rather than explain the candidate's own platform. I have to laugh at the back-and-forth of political television ads. It's not uncommon to watch one commercial that praises Candidate A for wanting to spend more on education than candidate B, only to be followed by another ad that warns voters not to vote for Candidate A, who is inevitably going to raise taxes. The whole truth is hidden, and the advertisements are aimed at what people want to hear, not reality.

News reports are similar. Filled with bad news and assumptions rather than simply sharing the facts, they oftentimes report a skewed version of the truth, one more pleasing to the general public. And the general population's voice is treated as fact too. Look at social media. The posted opinions are seen as fact rather than opinion—and everyone's opinions are considered fact!

When did culture stray so far from the truth? For that matter, what is truth?

Science creates truth. If you can prove something by observation, it must be true. But what about things that cannot be directly observed but still exist? Are they in fact not real? Often we need to see to believe, but how do you explain the wind? You can see the effects of the wind, but why does that prove it is wind and not just a dancing tree?

Is the Internet truth? If a relationship is not official until it is posted on Facebook, does that mean everything you read online is true? In college, my best friend decided to change his Facebook status to "engaged" rather than "in a relationship with." The fallout from that was funny from my perspective but caused concern for other people—mainly the girlfriend's mom. It was not true, but how could anyone know?

So where do you turn? How can you prove that the Bible is truth? Society will challenge you. They will use science in attempts to disprove many things, but God offers proof of His existence:

> The heavens declare the glory of God, and the sky above proclaims His handiwork. (Psalm 19:1)
>
> For His invisible attributes, namely, His eternal power and divine nature, have been clearly perceived, ever since the creation of the world, in the things that have been made. (Romans 1:20)

Everything in creation points to a Divine Creator, and we have His story in the Bible. The Bible is absolute truth—God's Word. The Bible proclaims a message of love and redemption. Is that so hard to believe?

We live in a time when perfection is expected but never a possibility. When someone messes up, the first response is discredit and dismissal rather than forgiveness and healing. The world is a critical place. No one is exempt from criticism.

God's Word is critical too. It demands obedience. It shares hard messages about the truth. But God also knows we are an imperfect people. The reality is that He sent His only Son to die on the cross for you (John 3:16). It no longer matters if you are perfect, because God is perfect. We are affirmed of this truth in 2 Samuel 22:31, "This God—His way is perfect;

the word of the LORD proves true; He is a shield for all those who take refuge in Him."

What more needs to be said? God is perfect and has a perfect love for you. He loves you even in your failures and proved His love by sending His Son to die for you. With many forces trying to disprove God, be an example of His love. He has already proven Himself and does not need us to fight a crusade. Just live in His love and reflect that amazing grace He displayed through Jesus. And even if you fail, don't fret. He forgives you. Let Him be your shield and take refuge in Him.

Reflection

Failure is truth in a world where success is a god. Failure is a reality in a world that defines reality as a twenty-first century television show. Failure is a blemish in a world polished by makeover specialists and spin doctors.

Considering that failure is something to live with, we need to give it a dose of God's reality. Failure began when truth failed—way back in the Garden of Eden days. Satan fabricated a fatal lie, which Eve believed and passed directly to Adam. The sad truth is that God's first children chose to believe the lie. They chose to disobey God. The first failure doomed all creation for all time.

And there were other truths, other realities, many of them dark stories of murder, deceit, assault, cheating, and rejecting God. The Old Testament often seems shrouded with failures, failures of the spiritual variety that resulted in broken lives lived as God never intended.

But still, there were more truths, more realities. Far more lasting and potent than all the sin was all the forgiveness. God's people never relented from sinning, and God never relented from forgiving. As Satan revealed the sins of God's people, God revealed His unconditional love.

This is more than a good story with a happy ending. It sets an example for life today—life in your family, among your friends, and within your occupational circles. Sadly, those who do not know the story of salvation revealed by God in both testaments of the Bible cannot begin to understand what it means to be God's people today. They expect to see perfection; instead, they see reality.

My family's cycle of reality is one of sin and forgiveness, imitating with far less drama than the cycles of God's people in relation to one another and to Him. Those outside the faith expect to see a perfect family; after all, we are among the few families in our neighborhood that leave the house every Sunday morning for worship and Bible class. We are a family of professional church workers. The reality is that we are not perfect. A persistent cycle of repentance and forgiveness defines us.

Do not allow your life as God's child to be defined by a nonbeliever's reality—or, for that matter, the reality of a believer who does not perceive the fullness of his or her salvation. Some believers think they must do something to be saved. They do not understand the truth that God has already done everything for their salvation.

The final reality is yet to come. You will experience the much-dreaded Judgment Day. Only you *don't* need to dread it. For you, a saved sinner, the reality is that you have already been judged. The truth is out. Your future reality is that you live in heaven with Jesus and all His beloved children. It will be one reality show that really is reality. And it will last a lot longer than sixty minutes.

52

A Matter of Perspective

2 Timothy 3:14–17

I like jigsaw puzzles. Each piece of the puzzle contributes to the overall picture. Some puzzles are simple to solve and others require patience and work. If you have ever completed a puzzle with another person, you encounter new challenges and new outlooks on how best to solve the puzzle.

Andie and I work well together on puzzles because we have similar strategies. We both agree that the border gets completed first, but other obvious fits are acceptable to piece together before we finish the border. Once the border is done, we each take an area based on color schemes, and once we get perplexed, we switch. Sometimes we experience adversity when we grow impatient, but, overall, we work well together to piece together a complicated project.

This book has been a fun experience to share with my dad. After I had completed some of the early chapters, I had wanted to go back and add something that popped in my head. Before I could do that, I checked his *Reflection* and found that he had already added it without knowing my intentions. As similar as our perspectives are, I found many of his reflections interesting. The completed project offered more insight and wisdom than either one of us could have offered alone.

Think about teachers and professors you have had. Did you learn better from some than you did from others? We are wired differently in the ways that we learn and in the ways we think. Because of our wiring and experiences, everyone has different perspectives. Some may share similar perspectives, and stronger relationships ensue. At other times, perspectives clash and you never see eye-to-eye with the other person. How do you see your perspectives influencing your attitude, relationships, or job?

Being able to step outside of your perspectives and look at obstacles or opportunities through the eyes of someone else can positively affect your outlook. Maybe your sister was offered a job far away. Would you look at that as a challenge rather than an opportunity? Do you know all the details involved or all the thought placed in the decision-making process? Her perspective is the only one that really matters, and it is important that you care, but it is more important for you to be understanding.

When you are faced with a challenge involving others, put yourself in their shoes. How do they view the situation? Different perspectives are just small parts of the whole. Few perspectives are automatically incorrect; they might just be incomplete. Artwork provides an example. Everyone has a valid perspective on a piece of art, but only the artist truly knows the full meaning behind their work of art. A piece of art can mean different things to different people, but only the artist can provide the real inspiration.

God is an artist. Beyond His masterpiece of creation, He supplies a beautiful manuscript that displays His art. Through John, He clearly defines the purpose: "But these are written so that you may believe that Jesus is the Christ, the Son of God, and that by believing you may have life in His name" (John 20:31).

The Artist starts in Genesis and promises a Savior. The rest of Scripture adds various different pieces to the puzzle of salvation to contribute the framework—the framework of Jesus. Maybe the accounts of the Old Testament help you believe in God. Maybe the Psalms or literary writings are more effective for you. No matter what lens helps you see most accurately, God wants you to believe in Him, and the Holy Spirit actively creates and nurtures your faith.

Perspectives can be troublesome when you discount the validity of other people's perspectives. Everyone has a perspective. It makes us unique individuals. When you rely on yourself, you are incomplete and risk failure. Trust in God's perspective as truth, and rely on Him. His love never fails, and His promises are fulfilled. He is the Artist who created you, and He loves His creation. You are valuable to Him!

I leave you with these words found in Paul's second letter to young Timothy:

> But as for you, continue in what you have learned and have firmly believed, knowing from whom you learned it and how from childhood you have been acquainted with the sacred writings, which are able to make you wise for salvation through faith in Christ Jesus. All Scripture is breathed out by God and profitable for teaching, for reproof, for correction, and for training in righteousness, that the man of God may be complete, equipped for every good work. (2 Timothy 3:14–17)

Reflection

I detest puzzles! Eight pieces or one thousand, I hate them equally. I have neither the patience nor the desire to piece together slips of cardboard designed by some malcontent to . . . to . . . to . . . well, to puzzle me to the point of frustration. (Can you tell that I do not like puzzles?)

I admire Aaron and Andie for their puzzle persistence. Were I to team with Renee for puzzle solutions, marital tensions would set a forty-plus-year relationship aquiver. Besides, she is good at puzzles and many other things that puzzle me. Scrabble. Gardening. Putting things together.

I hate puzzles—but I already said that!

Aaron and I working together on this book was a puzzle. When I write alone, I do not have to put pieces together. But as Aaron started each lesson, it was a puzzle that I had to complete. I do not like to work that hard. But I had to, and it was an experience that helped me to grow—as a writer, a teacher, and, yes, as a dad. You can grow from doing things that challenge you and make you work hard. This was one puzzle that I grew to love. I loved it because Aaron is my son.

I thank God that His story of salvation is not a puzzle to me. Aaron said that you cannot do certain things alone, and puzzles may be one of them. The Bible is another. It does not puzzle me because the Holy Spirit works with me. Okay, to be honest, the Spirit fits the pieces together, giving me a chance to see how all of God's Word works together in one piece. Forget Old Testament and New Testament; think *History of My Salvation*.

The story of Jesus puzzles many people. Who could be that loving? Who could be that perfect? Who could die and come back to life again? Who could defeat Satan and take away our sins?

Easy questions for you, right? God has been working on the puzzle with you too. God loves you because Jesus is His Son. He took away your sins. He put all the puzzle pieces together—and there you are, the completed picture of God's child.

God bless you as you learn life's lessons and grow in faith.